THE BIBLE

is a book of revelation that has inspired men throughout the centuries. It is also an unsurpassed history of some of the greatest empires and civilizations the world has known. No other volume offers so much history, biography and literature to its reader. But until recently many of the seeming contradictions and obscurities contained within the Bible were open only to individual interpretation.

The discovery of the Dead Sea Scrolls in the 1950's, important excavations in Palestine, and access to documents in former dead languages have cleared away many of these Biblical mysteries. Here at last is a unique guide which taps these new sources of research and fits newly discovered information into proper Biblical sequence and perspective. Mr. Schonfield, a widely influential and highly respected Bible expert, includes everything from natural geography to noted individuals . . . from A to Z . . . in this important and enlightening supplement to Bible reading.

READERS' A TO Z BIBLE COMPANION

Hugh J. Schonfield, D.S.Litt., F.I.A.L.

A SIGNET REFERENCE BOOK
PUBLISHED BY THE NEW AMERICAN LIBRARY,
NEW YORK AND TORONTO
THE NEW ENGLISH LIBRARY LIMITED, LONDON

FIRST PRINTING, DECEMBER, 1967

SIGNET TRADEMARK REG. U.S. PAT. OFF. AND FOREIGN COUNTRIES
REGISTERED TRADEMARK—MARCA REGISTRADA
HECHO EN CHICAGO, U.S.A.

SIGNET REFERENCE BOOKS are published
in the United States by
The New American Library, Inc.,
1301 Avenue of the Americas, New York, New York 10019
in Canada by The New American Library of Canada Limited,
295 King Street East, Toronto 2, Ontario,
in the United Kingdom by The New English Library Limited,
Barnard's Inn, Holborn, London, E.C. 1, England

PRINTED IN THE UNITED STATES OF AMERICA

CONTENTS

READERS' A TO Z BIBLE COMPANION

INTRODUCTION

No one who reads and knows the Bible can be described as an uneducated person, however little schooling he may have had. Not only does it offer spiritual guidance and illumination, it is a repository of the march of history from remote times, having to do with some of the greatest empires and civilizations the world has known. Within its compass are to be found venerable laws and customs, the life of town and country, notable biographies, songs and poems of great beauty, penetrating parables and proverbs—a whole range of subjects so artlessly brought before the mind as to constitute the highest art. What other single volume teaches so much so effortlessly?

But the wealth of the Bible in terms of human knowledge is now seen to be much more extensive than could be imagined a century or more ago. There were many terms and allusions in it, which for lack of background information had to be passed over with only partial comprehension. Much was mentioned of which the full significance could not be appreciated in the absence of illustrations of the manners, usages, and circumstances of the ancient East. Only since scholar and spade have combined to resurrect what was buried has it become increasingly possible to tap these hidden biblical resources. In galleries and museums we can inspect numerous relics of the past, which throw light on former obscurities, and we have access to records in former dead languages that furnish an amazing guide to and commentary upon events and conditions covered by the Book of Books.

Only an encyclopedia could do justice to the vast amount of material bearing on the contents of the Bible that has piled up as a result of chance finds and the excavation of archaeologists. This book is not of that order, though it has employed the contributions of many authorities in a variety of fields. Its aim, quite simply, is to be a companion to the intelligent reader of the Bible, sitting at his elbow, ready to assist him with explanations, extra information, and useful knowledge. It also is designed to bring into perspective the progression of persons and events in relation to what was going on in and around the Holy Land at each period. The literary aspects have only been touched upon lightly because these have been dealt with by the writer in a previous work, **A History of Biblical Literature** (Mentor Book MT 376, published by The New American Library.)

Inevitably, what has been included in the present volume is the result of selection, and choice has often proved extremely difficult. The writer had to propose for himself some guiding principle, which would not make his decisions merely arbitrary or based on personal interest and preference. What he has tried to include, therefore, has been what was less likely to be familiar and what the average reader might wish to know without having to search in libraries. Sometimes this may seem comparatively trivial information, but it may be of consequence in creating an image or giving added substance to an episode. The same principle has governed the determination of the subjects or themes of the different Parts. At a second stage of preparation a good deal of the text was trimmed and compressed, without, it is hoped, loss of any essentials, in order to make room for additional items omitted in the first draft.

Although the author has striven to be as comprehensive as was practicable in a handy volume, he has had to leave himself open to the criticism that this or that has been left out which ought to have been in or that the treatment of some momentous idea or circumstance is inadequate or misleading. The author can only apologize for his shortcomings, and stress particularly that his work seeks to be nonsectarian and free from bias. The term "reader" has been defined to embrace those of no religious persuasion as well as the followers of all the great faiths and in particular the adherents of all of the expressions of Judaism and Christianity to whom the Bible is a sacred and inspired volume. Beauty, it is said, is in the eye of the beholder, and surely this also is true of prejudice. Actually, what is chiefly controversial in this work lies in the domain of scholarly disagreement. Here the writer, qualifying his statements when there was evident uncertainty, has preferred to make a judgment helpful to the layman when strictly, and perhaps bewilderingly, he should have indicated various alternative opinions.

In selecting the material, a major concern was to avoid making the book a mixture of a directory and a descriptive catalogue of antiquities. Something must, therefore, be said about the arrangement. A structure has been achieved by giving the Parts a logical progression. In fact, they advance in pairs. The first pair of Parts deals with physical geography and natural history. With the next pair we come to peoples and places and an outline of history. With the following pair, the reader is brought more intimately into touch with social and economic life, and with laws, customs, and beliefs. The succeeding pair singles out notable individuals, and the final pair provides supplementary references. Wherever it could be done, in keeping with the design of the volume, the information is presented alphabetically as most convenient for consultation. A general index has not, therefore, been required, but the alphabetical lists could not embrace incidental references in the text, which did not otherwise figure specifically in one or another of the Parts. Accordingly, such references have been given an index at the end of the book as an additional guide to the contents.

It remains for me warmly to thank Mr. Michael Kotka for his assistance with research and to express the hope that the work will be of service in the study and teaching of the Bible.

HUGH J. SCHONFIELD

PART I

PHYSICAL GEOGRAPHY

Desert and Wilderness—Forests and Woods—Islands—Mountains and Hills—Plains—Rivers and Streams—Rocks, Caves, and Stones—Seas and Lakes—Springs, Wells, and Pools—Valleys and Divides

The world of the Bible is predominantly that of the region forming the junction of the continents of Europe, Asia, and Africa. It was well fitted by nature to be the cradle of great civilizations, because associated with a generous warmth of climate it possessed river systems that helped provide a sweeping arc of productive land ideal for settled habitation, appropriately described as the Fertile Crescent. The region also lent itself to the diffusion of culture and commerce by furnishing convenient routes of communication by land and sea. To the southwest was the river Nile, emptying its waters into the Mediterranean through channels that formed a rich, intensely cultivated delta. On the north and east were the Tigris and Euphrates, giving access to the Persian Gulf and creating a second great zone of cultivation in Mesopotamia—the land between the two rivers. In between was a corridor of territory enjoying good rainfall, bounded on the north by the river Orontes and the mountains of the Lebanon, on the west by the Mediterranean, and on the east by a depression coming down from Syria through the valley of the river Jordan and the Dead Sea to the Gulf of 'Aqaba and the Red Sea. It was part of this intermediate strip, acting as a highway between Egypt and Mesopotamia, which was destined to be known as the Holy Land. Desert, mountain, and sea impinged upon it, bringing periodic incursions of migrant virile peoples, movements of forces and cultures, disturbing, energizing, and stimulating, an alternation of overthrow and re-creation, so that life could never stagnate or be devoid of challenge.

DESERT AND WILDERNESS

In the King James Version of the Bible the word wilderness is used as the translation of several Hebrew words. The commonest of these, **midbar,** refers to areas not under cultivation, wild, rough, or rugged country, not necessarily lacking vegetation. Desert regions of sandy wastes were familiar to the south and east, but they figure little in the Bible story because they were not traversed to any extent by peoples moving slowly with flocks and herds. The principal wildernesses mentioned in the Bible lay on the west of the Dead Sea and to the south and southwest. The chief connection of the former is with the story of David when he was being hunted by King Saul. Various named wildernesses in this region are connected with the Wildernesses of Judah, where in New Testament times John the Baptist preached. There, too, the Essene community had its center, near the Dead Sea at a place now called Khirbet Qumran, close to the caves which housed its library. The latter wildernesses figure mainly in relation to the exodus of the Israelites from Egypt and their journeys on the way to the Promised Land. Some of the wildernesses took their names from adjacent towns. In the list which follows, those which have associations with the Wilderness of Judah are indicated by an asterisk, while those which have associations with the wanderings of the Israelites are indicated by a dagger.

***AI,** wilderness near (Josh. 8:15).

***BETH-AVEN,** Wilderness of (Josh. 18:12).

DAMASCUS, Wilderness of (I Kings 19:15).

***EDOM,** Wilderness of (II Kings 3:8).

***EN-GEDI,** Wilderness of (I Sam. 24:1).

***GIBEAH,** wilderness near (Judg. 20:42).

***JUDAH,** Wilderness of (Ref. not by name. Josh. 15:61; Mark 1:4, etc.).

†KADESH (KADESH-BARNEA), Wilderness of (Num. 33:36; Ps. 29:8).

***MAON,** Wilderness of (I Sam. 23:25).

***MICHMASH,** wilderness near (I Sam. 13:18).

†MOAB, Wilderness of (Num. 21:11; Deut. 2:8).

†PARAN, Wilderness of (Gen. 14:7, 21:21; Num. 10:12, 12:16, 13:3, 26; I Sam. 25:1).

†SHUR, Wilderness of (Exod. 15:22).

†SIN, Wilderness of (Exod. 16:1, 17:1).

†SINAI, Wilderness of (Num. 9:5, 10:12).

***TEKOA,** Wilderness of (II Chron. 20:20).

†ZIN, Wilderness of (Num. 33:36, Josh. 15:3).

***ZIPH,** Wilderness of (I Sam. 23:14, 26:2).

FORESTS AND WOODS

In ancient times Palestine and Syria were well wooded, having extensive forests, woods, and thickets, in which there was an abundance of wildlife. Part of the Jordan valley was a jungle. The common Hebrew term for forest in the Bible is

ya'ar (On Trees and Wild Animals, see Part II, NATURAL HISTORY.)

ARABIA, forest in (Isa. 21:13).

CARMEL, Forest of (II Kings 19:23).

EPHRAIM, Wood of, east of the Jordan (II Sam. 18:6).

FOREST OF THE SOUTH (Ezek. 20:46).

Forests in the mountains of Judah where King Jotham built forts (II Chron. 27:4).

HARETH, Forest of, in Judah (I Sam. 22:5).

KING'S FOREST, a royal timber reservation (Neh. 2:8).

LEBANON, Forest of, in Syria (II Kings 19:23). King Solomon built a royal lodge of cedar called the House of the Forest of Lebanon (I Kings 7:2).

Wood near Beth-Aven, where the Israelites gathered honey (I Sam. 14:25).

Wood on the way from Jericho to Bethel where bears attacked the children who mocked the Prophet Elisha (II Kings 2:24).

Wood in the wilderness of Ziph, where David took refuge (I Sam. 23:15).

ISLANDS

The mass of islands in the eastern Mediterranean are referred to collectively in the Old Testament as "the isles of the Gentiles" (Gen. 10:5), and more commonly as "the isles of the sea." The principal ones distinguished by name are Caphtor (possibly Crete), and Chittim (Cyprus). In the New Testament a number of islands are mentioned, chiefly in connection with the travels of St. Paul. These are indicated by an asterisk.

CAPHTOR (see **CRETE**), (Deut. 2:23; Amos 9:7).

***CAUDA (CLAUDA)**, small island south of Crete, now Gaudos (Acts 27:16).

***CHIOS**, west of Smyrna (Izmir), (Acts 20:15).

CHITTIM (see Cyprus), Phoenician colony, afterwards Greek **KITION** (Jer. 2:10, Ezek. 27:6).

***COOS (COS)**, small island southwest of Caria, birthplace of Hippocrates (Acts 21:1).

***CRETE**, ancient center of the Minoan civilization. According to the Bible, if Crete is identified with Caphtor, the place of origin of the Philistines (Acts 27:7; Titus 1:5).

***CYPRUS**, under Roman rule when Paul and Barnabas visited the island, landing at Salamis and preaching the Gospel to the governor Sergius Paullus at Paphos. Barnabas was a Levite from Cyprus (Acts 4:36, 13:4, etc.).

ELISHAH, Isles of, not identifiable, but connected with the Greeks (Ezek. 27:7).

***MELITA**, the modern Malta, where St. Paul was shipwrecked (Acts 28:1).

***MYTILENE**, capital of the island of **LESBOS**, birthplace of Sappho, (Acts 20:14).

PATMOS, southwest of Samos, where John who saw the Revelation was a prisoner (Rev. 1:9).

***RHODES**, famed for the huge statue of Apollo known as the Colossus; in the Middle Ages home of the Knights of St. John (Acts 21:1).

***SAMOS**, off the coast of Asia Minor southwest of Ephesus, noted for its pottery and wine (Acts 20:15).

***SAMOTHRACIA (SAMOTHRACE)**, in the northeast of the Aegean (Acts 16:11).

***TYRE (ZUR)**, ancient Phoenician city built on an island off the coast, finally connected to the mainland by Alexander the Great, noted for its purple dye. Hiram, king of Tyre, furnished timber, craftsmen, etc. to King Solomon (I Kings 9:11), etc.; Matt. 11:21, etc.).

MOUNTAINS AND HILLS

The mountainous area with which the Bible is chiefly concerned consists of the ranges of Syria and Palestine and of the Sinai peninsula. Northern Palestine is dominated by the Syrian ranges of the Lebanon and Anti-Lebanon, snow-capped and with a maximum altitude of over 10,000 feet. These continue south through Palestine and Jordan in lower ridges and hills separated by the cleft of the Jordan valley and the Dead Sea. The western ridge includes the highlands of Galilee, Mt. Tabor, and the mountains of Samaria and Judah, while the eastern ridge is represented by the mountains of Bashan, Moab and Edom. Ultimately the western ridge enters the Sinai peninsula, and passing down the western side of the Gulf of ‘Aqaba culminates in the mountainous region at the tip of the peninsula with its great peaks associated with the giving of the Ten Commandments.

Among ancient peoples the majesty and dignity of mountain and hilltops made them seem the natural habitat of gods and the places where they should be worshipped. The God of Israel, YHVH, seems originally to have been a mountain god. We therefore find holy mountains in the Bible and many references to pagan hill shrines and high places. Purer monotheism still retained some of this ancient veneration.

ABARIM, mountains of (Num. 33:47), near the plains of Moab east of the Jordan. The name derives from the passes which provided communication across the mountains.

AMMAH, a hill near Gibeon (II Sam. 2:24).

AMORITES, mountain of (Deut. 1:7), possibly part of the hill country east of the Arabah.

ARARAT, mountains of (Gen. 8:4). Assyrian, **Urartu.** The highlands of eastern Turkey in the region of Lake Van, where the Ark of Noah rested after the Flood.

BASHAN, hill of (Ps. 68:15), east of Jordan, southeast of the Sea of Galilee.

BETHEL, Mt. (I Sam. 13:2), north of Jerusalem.

CARMEL, Mt. (I Kings 18:19), overlooking the bay of Haifa, where Elijah contended with the priests of Baal.

EBAL, Mt. (Deut. 11:29), one of the mountains of "blessing and cursing" facing Mt. Gerizim near Nablus (Shechem).

EPHRAIM, Mt. (Josh. 17:15), hill country of central Palestine.

EPHRON, Mt. (Josh. 15:9), near Kiriath-Jearim west of Jerusalem.

GAREB, a hill near Jerusalem (Jer. 31:39).

GERIZIM, Mt. (Deut. 11:29). Holy mountain of the Samaritans. (See **EBAL.**)

GILBOA, Mt. (I Sam. 31:1), west of Beth-Shan, overlooking the eastern end of the plain of Jezreel, where Saul and Jonathan were killed in battle with the Philistines.

GILEAD, Mt. (Gen. 31:21), east of the Jordan.

HACHILAH, hill of (I Sam. 23:19), west of the Dead Sea.

HALAK, Mt., "the bare mountain" in the south (Josh. 11:17).

HERES, Mt. (Judg. 1:35).

HERMON, Mt. (9,232 ft.) in Syria. Highest in the Anti-Lebanon; always snow-covered (Deut. 3:8-9, 4:48). Called by the Sidonians Sirion (Sion) and by the Amorites Senir (Shenir).

HOR, Mt. (Num. 20:22), in the wilderness of Kadesh northeast of Kadesh-Barnea where Aaron, first high priest of Israel, died.

HOREB, Mt. (Exod. 3:1), apparently identical with Mt. Sinai as the "mountain of God" in the Sinai peninsula west of the Gulf of 'Aqaba; but the situation and identification are disputed.

ISRAEL, mountain of (Josh. 11:16).

JEARIM, Mt. associated with a Mt. Seir west of Jerusalem (Josh. 15:10).

JUDAH, mountains of (Josh. 11:21).

LEBANON, Mt. (Judg. 3:3).

MARS HILL, or Areopagus (hill of Ares, god of war), at Athens. Where St. Paul addressed the Court of Areopagus (Acts 17).

MOREH, hill of, south of Mt. Tabor (Judg. 7:1).

MORIAH, Mt. (II Chron. 3:1), one of the hills of Jerusalem on which Solomon built the Temple, traditionally associated with Abraham's offering of his son Isaac (Gen. 22:2).

NAPHTALI, Mt. (Josh. 20:7).

NEBO, Mt. (Deut. 34:1), east of the exit of the Jordan into the Dead Sea, where Moses died, named from a Moabite god (Babylonian, **Nabu**).

OLIVES, Mt. of (**OLIVET**), on the east of Jerusalem (Zech. 14:4; Matt. 21:1).

PARAN, Mt. (Deut. 33:2). Probably so-called from the Wilderness of Paran of which the Wilderness of Sinai was the southern part, and thus an alternative name for Mt. Sinai, scene of the giving of the Law.

PEOR, (Num. 23:28), hill in Moab east of the Jordan, a high place of the god Baal of Peor from which the soothsayer Balaam delivered an oracle on Israel.

PISGAH, (Deut. 34:1), an elevation associated with Mt. Nebo from which Moses surveyed the Promised Land. (See **NEBO.**)

SAMARIA, mountains of (Jer. 31:5) in central Palestine, also Hill of Samaria owned by Shermer on which the capital of the kingdom of Israel was built by Omri (I Kings 16:24).

SEIR, Mt. (Gen. 36:8) in the land of the Edomites southwest of the Dead Sea, home of Esau; also of a hill near Kiriath-Jearim (Josh. 15:10).

SENIR (SHENIR). (See **HERMON.**)

SEPHAR, described as a mountain of the east (Gen. 10:30).

SHEPHER (SHAPHER), Mt., a stopping place in the wanderings of the Israelites (Num. 33:23).

SINAI, Mt. (Exod. 19:11; Gal. 2:24), scene of the giving of the Law to Moses. Perhaps either Jebel Musa (7,370 ft.) or Jebel Serbal (6,825 ft.) in the Sinai peninsula, but identification is uncertain. (See **HOREB.**)

SIRION (SION). (See **HERMON.**)

TABOR, Mt. (Judg. 4:6), rounded mountain on the edge of the Plain of Esdraelon, ancient religious high place. Traditional scene of the transfiguration of Jesus.

ZALMON, Mt. (Judg. 9:48), near Shechem.

ZEMARAIM, Mt. (II Chron. 13:4), north of Jerusalem.

ZION, Mt. (II Kings 19:31), one of the hills of Jerusalem on which was an ancient Jebusite fort. This southeastern hill became the site of the Temple built by Solomon. Zion is extolled by the Hebrew poets and prophets. (See also **MORIAH.**)

PLAINS

No less than seven different Hebrew words in the Old Testament are translated by the word plain in the King James Version. Only two of these, **biqah** and **mishor,** relate to flat country of any extent. The word **shephelah** describes the lowlands of the Mediterranean coastal zone, while the **arabah** is the arid region of the Dead Sea depression and southwards. **Kikkar** speaks of the "curving" course chiefly of the Jordan valley, while **abel** (once only) means a meadow. **Elon** should be rendered oak tree, e.g., "the oak of Moreh" not "plain of Moreh." The plain of Jezreel (Esdraelon), running southeast from Carmel, is referred to as the Valley of Jezreel. Part of this is the plain of Megiddo, a **biqah** translated as valley. The actual coastal plain between Joppa (Jaffa) and Caesarea is called **Sharon,** which means "the plain." In the following list the first two letters of each of the Hebrew words is set beside the references to identify the type of country.

AVEN, plain (**bi**) of (Amos 1:5).

DURA, plain (**bi**) of (Dan. 3:1) in Babylonia.

JERICHO, plains (**ar**) of (Josh. 4:13), north of the Dead Sea.

JERUSALEM, plain country (**ki**) round (Neh. 12:28).

JORDAN, plain (**ki**) of (Gen. 13:10), the lower Jordan valley.

MAMRE, plain (**el**) of (Gen. 13:18), actually oak tree.

MEDEBA, plain (**mi**) of (Josh. 13.9), in northern Moab east of the Jordan.

MEONENIM, plain (**el**) of (Judg. 9:37), actually oak tree.

MOAB, plains (**ar**) of (Num. 22:1), as **MEDEBA.**

MOREH, plain (**el**) of (Gen. 12:6), actually oak tree.

PHILISTINES, plain (**sh**) of (Obad. 19), the lower coastal plain.

SHINAR, plain (**bi**) of (Gen. 11:2), in Mesopotamia.

TABOR, plain (**el**) (I Sam. 10:3), near Bethel, actually oak tree.

ZAANAIM, plain (**el**) of (Judg. 4:11), actually oak tree.

Additional Level Tracts

JERICHO, valley (**bi**) of (Deut. 34:3).

LEBANON, valley (**bi**) of (Josh. 11:17), between the Lebanon and Anti-Lebanon.

MEGIDDO, valley (**bi**) of (II Chron. 35:22).

MIZPEH, valley (**bi**) of (Josh. 11:8).

SHARON (I Chron. 17:29), the fertile coastal plain north of Jaffa.

SHEPHELAH (tr. valley), the lower coastal plain (Deut. 1:17).

RIVERS AND STREAMS

The great rivers of the Bible are the Nile, the Tigris, the Euphrates and the Jordan. The Nile is not mentioned by name: it is referred to as "the River," but an eastern arm is called Sihor. The "river of Egypt" several times mentioned is not the Nile but the Rhinocorura on the border between Egypt and Palestine. The Euphrates is also sometimes called simply "the River" or "the Great River." Canals of Babylonia like the Chebar are described as rivers. Where a river flowed in a seasonal watercourse it is commonly differentiated by the word **nachal** instead of **nahar.** Occasionally **nachal** is translated brook.

Among rivers of Palestine not specifically mentioned in the Bible are the Yarmuk, an eastern tributary of the Jordan south of the Sea of Galilee, and the Auja (now Yarkon) entering the Mediterranean at the modern town of Tel-Aviv. In the New Testament the life of St. Paul was associated with great cities which were on the banks of rivers, though these are not named. They include the Cydnus at Tarsus, the Cayster at Ephesus, the Orontes at Antioch in Syria, and the Tiber at Rome.

ABANA (AMANA), one of the rivers of Damascus (II Kings 5:12).

AHAVA, river of, probably a canal in Babylonia (Ezra 8:15).

ARNON, described as both river and brook (Deut. 2:24), the Wadi Mojib flowing into the Dead Sea on the eastern side.

BESOR, Brook (I Sam. 30:9).

CHEBAR, river of (Ezek. 1:3), the Kabari Canal at Nippur in Babylonia where the prophet Ezekiel saw a vision of God.

CHERITH, Brook, associated with the prophet Elijah (I Kings 27:3), flowing into the Jordan on the eastern side.

EGYPT, river of (Num. 34:5), the Rhinocorura (Wadi el 'Arish) flowing into the Mediterranean south of Gaza.

ESHCOL, Brook (Num. 13:23).

EUPHRATES (Hebrew, **Perath**), one of the rivers of Mesopotamia, also associated with the Garden of Eden (Gen. 2:14; Rev. 9:14).

GAASH, brooks of (II Sam. 23:30).

GAD, river of (II Sam. 24:5).

GIHON, river associated with the Garden of Eden (Gen. 2:13).

GOZAN, river of (see **HABOR**).

HABOR, River, same as river of Gozan (II Kings 17:6), tributary of the Euphrates above Mari, now called Khabur.

HIDDEKEL (see **TIGRIS**).

JABBOK, tributary of the Jordan on the east (Gen. 32:22), where Jacob wrestled with the angel, now called Nahr ez Zerka.

JORDAN, River (Gen. 22:10), flowing into the Dead Sea, where Jesus was baptized (Mark 1:9).

KANAH. River (Josh. 16:8), now Wadi Qana.

KIDRON (KEDRON), Brook (II Sam. 15:23; John 18:1), in the valley between Jerusalem and the Mount of Olives.

KISHON, River (Judg. 4:7), flowing into the Mediterranean north of Haifa, modern Nahr el Muqatta.

NILE, known in the Bible as **ye'or** (the River), Egyptian, **Hapi** (Gen. 41:1).

PERATH (see **EUPHRATES**).

PHARPAR, one of the rivers of Damascus (II Kings 5:12).

PISHON (PISON), river associated with the Garden of Eden (Gen. 2:11).

SIHOR (SHIHOR), an eastern branch of the Nile, from the Egyptian name meaning 'water of Horus' (Josh. 13:3).

TIGRIS, River of Mesopotamia, associated with the Garden of Eden (Gen. 2:14), called **HIDDEKEL.**

ULAI, river of (Dan. 8:2), flowing east of the Persian royal city of Susa (Shushan).

YARKON, the Wadi el Auja, flowing into the Mediterranean at Tel-Aviv, not mentioned in the Bible.

YARMUK, Greek **Hieromax,** enters the Jordan from the east just south of the Sea of Galilee, not named in the Bible.

ZERED, Brook (Deut. 2:13), flows into the south end of the Dead Sea, now called Wadi el Hesy.

ROCKS, CAVES, AND STONES

Geologically, Palestine is a rocky country with large areas of limestone and sandstone. Crags and outcrops of rock abound, often curiously shaped by wind, weather and sandstorm, forming memorable landmarks. Cliffs are honeycombed with caves, which served in many cases as regular habitations and were places of hiding and refuge in times of conflict. Rocks provided welcome shade, means of safety and defense, and a sense of permanence and solidarity. It was natural, therefore, that God should be described as the Rock, and that rock should figure as an enduring foundation. The setting up of monoliths and stone circles featured in ancient religion from the most remote times. The references which follow relate only to natural formations named in the Bible, excluding those erected by human hands such as at Bethel and Gilgal.

ADULLAM, Cave of, where David took refuge from Saul (I Sam. 22:1).

ADUMMIM, Ascent of, named from the red limestone, on the way from Jericho to Jerusalem (Josh. 15:7).

AKRABBIM, Ascent of, the 'Ascent of Scorpions' southwest of the Dead Sea (Num. 34:4).

BETH-SHEMESH, Great Stone at, where the Ark rested when it was returned by the Philistines (I Sam. 6:14).

BOHAN, Stone of, in the wilderness south-west of Jericho (Josh. 15:6).

BOZEZ, a sharp rock between Gibeah and Michmash, mentioned with another called **SENEH** (I Sam. 14:4).

ETAM, Rock, where Samson stayed (Judg. 15:8).

GIBEON, Great Stone at, to the north of Jerusalem (II Sam. 20:8).

GUR, Ascent of, where Ahaziah king of Judah was killed (II Kings 9:27).

MACHPELAH. Cave of, close to Hebron, place of burial of the Hebrew patriarchs, and of their wives except Rachel second wife of Jacob, purchased by Abraham to bury Sarah (Gen. 23:9).

MAKKEDAH, Cave at (Josh. 10:16).

OREB, Rock, where Gideon defeated and killed a Midianite prince called Oreb (Judg. 7:25).

RIMMON, Rock of, where the Benjamites fled from Israel (Judg. 20:45).

SENEH (see **BOZEZ**).

ZIZ, Ascent of, scene of a battle in which Jehoshaphat, king of Judah, defeated the forces of Ammon and Moab (II Chron. 20:16).

ZOHELETH, Stone of, close to En-Rogel at Jerusalem, where Adonijah conspired against his father King David (I Kings 1:9).

SEAS AND LAKES

Shipping in the ancient world provided a most important means of migration, travel and trade. The Mediterranean linked with the east the long southern seaboard of Europe and the opposite coasts of north Africa, and through the straits of Gibraltar (Pillars of Hercules) vessels passed out into the Atlantic, coasting down west Africa and voyaging north to the British Isles. By means of the arms of the Red Sea and the Persian Gulf, the east coast of Africa was explored and the coasts of Arabia, while points of Asia were reached across the Indian Ocean. Numerous accounts have come down to us of considerable voyages by Egyptians, Greeks, Phoenicians and Carthaginians. The history of nations was considerably affected by colonizing movements such as those of the "Peoples of the Sea" and by naval battles (see PART VIII).

The Bible has much to tell of those who "go down to the sea in ships," the Atlantic-going vessels of Tarshish, the navies of King Solomon sailing from Ezion-Geber "doing business in great waters," the seaborne invasion of Philistines from Caphtor. The New Testament shows how much shipping contributed to the missionary journeys of St. Paul, and offers a vivid description of storm and shipwreck in the account of his last voyage to Rome. The prophecy of the doom of Rome (Great Babylon) in Revelation 18 paints a brilliant word-picture of the wealth brought by sea to the Mistress of the World. The list of waters named in the Bible is, however, very limited.

ADRIA, ADRIATIC, Sea of, the central Mediterranean as well as the sea east of Italy (Acts 27:27).

AEGEAN (not named), but concerned in the reference to "islands of the sea" (Isa. 11:11) and to many places visited by St. Paul (Acts).

'AQABA, Gulf of (not named), but concerned in the reference to the ships of Solomon sailing from Elat and Ezion-Geber (I Kings 9:26f).

CHINNEROTH, CHINNERETH, the Sea of Galilee in the Old Testament (Josh. 12:3).

DEAD SEA (see **SALT SEA**).

EGYPTIAN SEA, Gulf of Suez (Isa. 11:15).

GALILEE, Sea or Lake of (Matt. 4:18; Luke 5:1), 13 miles long by 7½ miles wide and 700 feet below sea level, also known as the Sea of **TIBERIAS** (John 21:1).

GREAT SEA, the Mediterranean (Num. 34:6).

JOPPA, Sea of, the southeastern part of the Mediterranean (Ezra 3:7), also known as the Sea of the **PHILISTINES** (Exod. 23:31).

MEROM, Waters of, Lake Huleh through which the Jordan flowed before entering the Sea of Galilee (Josh. 11:5), now drained.

PHILISTINES, Sea of (see **JOPPA**).

RED SEA (Hebrew, Sea of Reeds), relating to the gulfs of Suez and 'Aqaba which embrace the Sinai peninsula. It has been suggested that the Sea of Reeds in the story of the Exodus from Egypt (Exod. 13:18) may be the Mediterranean coastal lake east of the Nile Delta (Lake Sirbonis).

SALT SEA (Gen. 14:3), also Sea of the Plain (Deut. 3:17), the Dead sea (Lake Asphaltis of the Greeks), 53 miles long by maximum 10 miles wide and 1290 feet below sea level.

TIBERIAS, Sea of (see **GALILEE**).

SPRINGS, WELLS, AND POOLS

The importance of water supplies in the Near East needs no stressing. Towns and villages were to be found where natural springs existed, as illustrated in the list below of place-names commencing with EN- (Spring or Fountain). In drier areas like the Negev, however, and with larger cities, it was essential to conserve water by the creation or development of rock pools and cisterns, and in later times by the construction of pipes and aqueducts. Some of these have lasted for thousands of years. Wells were dug wherever practicable. The Bible tells that notable romances began at wells where the women came to draw water, and there was also many a conflict over watering rights for cattle. We may quote an interesting passage in Genesis (26:18): "And Isaac digged again the wells of water, which they had digged in the days of Abraham his father; for the Philistines had stopped them after the death of Abraham; and he called their names after the names by which his father Abraham had called them." Among the gates of Jerusalem we find the Well or Fountain Gate (Neh. 2:14) and the Water Gate (Neh. 3:26).

The following places are identified by name with springs: **EN-AIM** or **EN-AM** (Gen. 38:14; Josh. 15:34), **EN-DOR** (Josh. 17:11), **EN-EGLAIM** (Ezek. 47:10), **EN-GANNIM** (Josh. 19:21), **EN-GEDI** (Josh. 15:62), **EN-HADDAH** (Josh. 19:37), **EN-HAZOR** (Josh. 19:37), **EN-MISHPAT** (Gen. 14:7) also known as Kadesh, **EN-NUN, AENON** (John 3:23), **EN-RIMMON** (Josh. 15:32), **EN-ROGEL** (Josh. 15:7), **EN-SHEMESH** (Josh. 15:7), **EN-TAPPUAH** (Josh. 17:7).

BEER-ELIM, site of a well (Isa. 15:8).

BEER-LAHAI-ROI, associated with story of Hagar (Gen. 16:14).

BEEROTH, Wells (Deut. 10:6).

BEER-SHEBA (Gen. 21:31).

BETHESDA (BETHZATHA), pool of, at Jerusalem where Jesus cured an impotent man (John 5:2).

BETH-LEHEM, well of (II Sam. 23:15–16).

DRAGON WELL, better rendered Jackal's Well (Neh. 2:13).

ELIM, twelve springs at (Exod. 15:27).

ESEK, well at (Gen. 16:20).

GIBEON, pool at (II Sam. 2:13).

GIHON, fountain and pool at (I Kings 1:33; II Chron. 32:30).

HEBRON, pool at (II Sam. 4:12).

HESHBON, fishpools in (Song of Sol. 7:4).

JACOB'S WELL, where Jesus conversed with a woman of Samaria (John 4:6).

KING'S POOL (Neh. 2:14).

MARAH, bitter waters at (Exod. 15:23).

MASSAH and **MERIBAH,** where water gushed from the rock at Horeb when struck by Moses (Exod. 17:6).

NEPHTOAH, well of the waters of (Josh. 18:15).

OLD POOL, at Jerusalem (Isa. 22:11).

REHOBOTH WELL (Gen. 26:22).

SAMARIA, pool of (I Kings 22:38).

SHILOAH, waters of (Isa. 8:6), same as **SILOAH.**

SILOAH (SILOAM), pool of, fountain in the valley by Jerusalem (Neh. 3:15–16; John 9:7).

SIRAH, pool of (II Sam. 3:26).

SITNAH, well at (Gen. 26:21).

SOLOMON'S POOLS (not named in Bible), in the valley of Etam (Urtas) near Bethlehem (II Chron. 11:6; Eccles. 2:6), supplied water to Jerusalem.

UPPER POOL at Jerusalem (II Kings 28:17).

VALLEYS AND DIVIDES

Palestine as a country of many hills naturally has a profusion of valleys, hollows, gorges and ravines. A certain number of these, not always the most distinctive, are named in the Bible. The more level spaces between hills rendered into English as valley have already been mentioned in the list of Additional Level Tracts in the section on Plains (see p. 21). Those valleys which are listed below come under the headings of their Hebrew terms, *Emek* (a low place), *Ge* (a hollow) and *Nachal* (a wadi).

Emek

ACHOR, Valley of, south of Jericho where Achan was stoned (Josh. 7:24).

AJALON (AIJALON), Valley of, where Joshua defeated the Amorites (Josh. 10:12).

BACA (Weeping), Valley of (Ps. 84:6).

BERACHAH (Blessing), Valley of, west of Tekoa, where Judah defeated Ammon and Moab (II Chron. 20:26).

DECISION, Valley of, symbolic name given to a valley outside Jerusalem, probably that of Jehoshaphat (Joel 3:14).

ELAH (Terebinth), Valley of, southwest of Jerusalem where David encountered Goliath the Philistine (I Sam. 17:2).

GIANTS, Valley of (see **REPHAIM,** Valley of).

GIBEON, Valley of (Isa. 28:21).

HEBRON, Valley of (Gen. 37:14).

JEHOSHAPHAT, Valley of, between Jerusalem and the Mt. of Olives (Joel 3:2).

JEZREEL, Valley of, part of the plain of Esdraelon (Josh. 27:16).

KEZIZ, Valley of (Josh. 18:21).

KING'S DALE (see **SHAVEH,** Valley of).

REPHAIM, Valley of, translated Valley of Giants (Josh. 15:8; II Sam. 5:18).

SHAVEH, Valley of, near Jerusalem where Abraham met the king of Sodom (Gen. 14:17).

SIDDIM, Valley of, southern part of the Dead Sea area where an alliance of kings of Mesopotamia defeated the five rulers of the region (Gen. 14:3).

SUCCOTH, Valley of, part of the Jordan Valley (Ps. 60:7).

Ge

CHARASIM (Craftsmen), Valley of (I Chron. 4:14; Neh. 11:35).

HAMON-GOG (Multitude of Gog), Valley of, symbolic name given to the Valley of Passengers, because prophetically the forces of Gog would perish there (Ezek. 39:11).

IPHTAHEL (JIPTHAH-EL), Valley of (Josh. 19:14).

MOUNTAINS, Valley of, near Jerusalem (Zech. 14:5).

PASSENGERS, Valley of (see **HAMON-GOG**).

SALT, Valley of, at the southern end of the Dead Sea, scene of battles with the Edomites (II Sam. 8:13).

SLAUGHTER, Valley of, symbolic name for the Valley of the **SON OF HINNOM** (Jer. 7:32).

SON OF HINNOM, Valley of, on the south of Jerusalem. Ancient place of sacrifice of children to Moloch by fire, which gave its name to the conception of Hell (**Ge-Hinnom,** Gehenna) in New Testament times (Josh. 15:8; II Chron. 28:3; Matt. 5:22).

VISION, Valley of, symbolic name for part of Jerusalem (Isa. 22:1).

ZEBOIM (Hyenas), Valley of, northeast of Jerusalem (I Sam. 13:18).

ZEPHATHAH, Valley of (II Chron. 14:10).

To these should be added the Fat (or Fertile) Valley (**Ge-Shemanim**) mentioned in Isa. 28:1. This name is read in the Old Hebrew of Matt. 26:36, agreeing with the Old Syriac **Gu-semani** and some Greek manuscripts **Gesamanei** or **Gessemanei,** as the place where was the garden in which Jesus was arrested. It may be more correct than Gethsemane, understood as representing a Hebrew **Gath-shemen** (olive press). Within Jerusalem running north and south was a valley known as the Tyropoeon, or Valley of Cheesemakers.

Nachal

ESHCOL, Valley of (Num. 32:9).

GERAR, Valley of (Gen 26:17).

KIDRON (CEDRON), Valley of, southeast of Jerusalem (John 18:1).

SHITTIM (Acacias), Valley of (Joel 3:18).

SOREK, Valley of, home of Delilah with whom Samson fell in love (Judg. 16:4).

ZARED (ZERED), Valley of, in Moab southeast of the Dead Sea (Num. 21:12).

PART II

NATURAL HISTORY

Birds—Domesticated Animals—Fish and Reptiles—Insects and Small Creatures—Plants and Trees—Wild Animals

The identification of the biblical fauna and flora has presented many difficulties, and certainly in all cases may never be achieved. But it is now possible to provide a substantially accurate listing. Sometimes a single word covers a number of varieties of a species. So far as they can be known, and the fauna and flora still exist, a collection has been assembled in the Biblical Zoo at Jerusalem.

In the arrangements of this Part, the index name is usually that of the King James Version, corrected where necessary in the description in the light of available information. Creatures in the Bible are distinguished as clean and unclean, the former only being permitted for food.

BIRDS

The names of the unclean birds, chiefly birds of prey, are given in Lev. 11:13–19. Doves and pigeons were the only birds used as sacrifices.

BITTERN (Isa. 14:23). Still known in the Middle East. Modern authorities translate the Hebrew word **qippod** as hedgehog or porcupine; but if this is correct the association with birds as in Isa. 34:11, and Zeph. 2:14 is rather incongruous. The name indicates a habit of drawing in the head.

COCK AND HEN (Matt. 23:37; not mentioned in the Old Testament). The domestic fowl was introduced into Palestine by the Persians after the Jews returned from the Babylonian Exile.

CORMORANT (Lev. 11:17). This bird is called in Hebrew **shalak.** Another bird called **qaath** (Isa. 34:11) is also translated cormorant, which some authorities take to be the pelican, and others a kind of hawk or vulture.

CRANE (Isa. 38:14). The crane was familiar in Palestine, but the Hebrew **sus** thus translated is held to be the swallow or swift.

CUCKOO (Lev. 11:16). Common in Palestine, but the Hebrew **shachaph** is held to be the sea gull or sea mew.

DOVE (Gen. 8:8; Matt. 3:16). The same word **yonah** in Hebrew serves for dove and pigeon, and it is not possible to distinguish which is intended. Another word **tor** (Gen. 15:9) represents the turtle dove.

DUCK, not named in the Bible, but no doubt known because common in Egypt.

EAGLE (Lev. 11:13). Different kinds of eagle were familiar in Palestine. The Hebrew word **nesher** is held to represent the great griffon vulture (Mic. 1:16; Matt. 24:28).

FATTED FOWL (I Kings 4:23), probably refers to geese common in Egypt.

GIER-EAGLE (Lev. 11:18). The Egyptian vulture.

GLEDE (Deut. 14:13). The Hebrew **raah** probably means the buzzard.

GOOSE (see **FATTED FOWL).**

HAWK (Lev. 11:16).

HERON (Lev. 11:19).

KITE (Lev. 11:14). Common in Palestine, but the Hebrew **ayyah** may also mean the falcon.

LAPWING (Lev. 11:19). The bird meant is the hoopoe.

NIGHT HAWK (Lev. 11:16). Possibly the nightjar.

OSPREY (Lev. 11:13).

OSSIFRAGE (Lev. 11:13). Possibly the bearded vulture.

OSTRICH (Lam. 4:3). The same Hebrew word **yeenim** is wrongly translated owl in Lev. 11:16 and elsewhere. Another word **chasidah,** translated ostrich in Job 39:13, may be the white stork (see **STORK**).

OWL, GREAT (Lev. 11:17). Probably the Egyptian eagle owl, but some authorities suggest the ibis. A different Hebrew word is also translated great owl in Isa. 34:15.

OWL, LITTLE (Lev. 11:17).

OWL, SCREECH (Isa. 34:14). Probably the tawny owl.

PARTRIDGE (I Sam. 26:20). Probably the ptarmigan.

PEACOCK (I Kings 10:22).

PELICAN (Lev. 11:18).

PIGEON (see **DOVE**).

QUAIL (Exod. 16:11–13).

RAVEN (Gen. 8:7).

SPARROW (Ps. 84:3; Matt. 10:29). Sometimes translated simply as bird or fowl.

STORK (Lev. 11:19), white and black varieties.

SWALLOW (Ps. 84:3). The Hebrew word is **deror.** Another word **sus** is probably the swift (see **CRANE**).

SWAN (Lev. 11:18). Some authorities translate water hen. Others think a species of owl is meant.

VULTURE (Lev. 11:14). Probably the black kite.

DOMESTICATED ANIMALS

Flocks and herds were a primary source of wealth in Biblical times, and consequently a common word for cattle was **miqneh** (property). They consisted of oxen, and sheep and goats called small cattle. Only clean animals, those which part the hoof and chew the cud, might be used for food. Oxen and asses were used for plowing and transport, but they might not be used together (Deut. 22:10). Hybridization was not permitted (Lev. 22:24). The Israelites did not therefore breed mules, though these were employed, probably imported from Egypt. In the Old Testament period, lambs and kids were often treated as pets, and to some extent dogs also, though more commonly in New Testament times. The cat is nowhere mentioned in the Bible, but as both cats and dogs were domesticated in the Roman Empire, and this was familiar to the Rabbis, the lack of reference to the cat does not mean that it was rare in Palestine. Possibly cats were not popular with Jews while their worship by the Egyptians (Bast) was of consequence.

APE (I Kings 10:22). Apes and monkeys were not native to Palestine, but were imported, probably from India and Ceylon, to be kept as pets by kings and princes. From Talmudic sources we learn that apes were trained to perform certain menial tasks. The baboon was sacred among the Egyptians.

ASS (Gen. 49:11; Matt. 21:2). Used for riding, plowing, and as a beast of burden. Eminent persons rode on white asses.

CAMEL (Gen. 12:16). Its hair was woven into cloth (Matt. 3:4).

CAT (not mentioned in the Bible), domesticated among the Egyptians, Greeks and Romans, and sacred in Egypt to the goddess Bast.

COW (Isa. 7:21), sacred in Egypt to the goddess Hathor.

DOG (Exod. 11:17; Matt. 7:6). Dogs were used mainly as scavengers, for protecting sheep and as watch dogs (**cave canem**). In general the dog was regarded as a degraded animal and the term dog was one of contempt; but the puppy was a pet in homes (Matt. 15:26–27).

DROMEDARY (Isa. 60:6), the swift-traveling camel. The Hebrew words translated dromedary in I Kings 4:28 and Esther 8:10 relate to fleet horses.

ELEPHANT (I Macc. 1:16). Elephant tusks were imported for the ivory (I Kings 10:22), and elephants may have been seen in Palestine in the Persian period. There is no reference to them, however, until the time of the Seleucid kings of Syria, who used them in battle with wooden turrets on their backs holding armed men. Maccabean coins are extant depicting the elephant.

GOAT (Gen. 15:9). Commonest of biblical domestic animals. It provided meat, milk and cheese; its hair was woven into material for curtains and tents, and its skin used for clothing, leather, and many other purposes.

GREYHOUND (Prov. 30:31). The reference is incorrect, but the meaning of the Hebrew word is uncertain.

HORSE (Gen. 47:17; Jas. 3:3). Horses were mainly used for hunting and warfare, and not in agriculture. Solomon was a keen breeder of horses. In Roman times they were widely employed for travel and sport (chariot racing).

MONKEY (see APE).

MULE (II Sam. 13:29). The breeding of mules was forbidden under the law of Lev. 22:24; but they were in use in the reign of King David, and it may be assumed that they were imported.

OXEN (Gen. 12:16), used in plowing and as draft animals, and for the treading of corn, etc.

SHEEP (Gen. 4:2).

SWINE (Lev. 11:7; Matt. 7:6). Among the Israelites swine were unclean animals and were not bred, but were in domestic use by other peoples in Palestine.

FISH AND REPTILES

Fish was an important article of diet and commerce, being found in abundance in the Mediterranean, the Sea of Galilee, and the River Jordan. The laws of Israel distinguished between clean and unclean fish, the former being those with fins and scales (Lev. 11:9). The Bible makes no attempt to name species of fish, commonly describing them in terms of size. Shellfish, while not eaten by the Hebrews, furnished the pearl, purple dye from the murex, and an ingredient of frankincense. Among fresh and salt water fish known, but not named in the Bible, were bream, carp, catfish, eel, herring, musht, perch, spanish mackerel, sprat, sturgeon, tonguefish, triton, and tunny. The larger sea creatures included the dolphin, dugong, seal, shark and whale. The Biblical references to reptiles are more specific, with some puzzles like the Dragon and Leviathan.

ADDER, ASP. The Old Testament has four words which are translated adder, one of these being also translated asp. The Hebrew words are **akshub,** either asp or viper (Ps. 140:3), **peten** translated asp in Deut. 32:33 and adder in Ps.58:4, which may be the Egyptian cobra, **tsiphoni** (Prov. 23:32) the greater viper, which is rendered cockatrice in Isa. 11:8 and elsewhere, and finally **shephiphon** (Gen. 49:17), the horned cerastes.

CHAMELEON (Lev. 11:30). One of the Hebrew words in this verse probably means the chameleon, but perhaps not the word so translated. Some authorities understand the chameleon where the King James Version reads mole. The word **koach** rendered chameleon may be the gecko or the monitor lizard (see also **LIZARD**).

COCKATRICE (Isa. 11:8), probably a kind of viper.

CROCODILE (see **DRAGON** and **LEVIATHAN**).

DRAGON (Rev. 12:3). This is the mythological type of monster, which may also be the implication in some of the Old Testament references. In others we should understand the crocodile and in certain instances a land or sea creature with long jaws, a large lizard, serpent, or shark, according to the context. Jackal has also been proposed for some passages.

FROG (Exod. 8:2).

GREAT FISH (Jonah 1:17). This is assumed to be the whale, because in the reference to Jonah in Matt. 12:40 the Greek word **ketos** is so translated. But the meaning is a sea monster, which might equally be a species of shark (see also **WHALE**).

LEVIATHAN (Job 41:1). The probabilities are that this monster of the deep represents the sea serpent with mythological associations. As with one reference to the Great Dragon the power of Egypt may be alluded to by this name in Isa. 27:1.

LITTLE FISH (Matt. 15:34). Many species in the Sea of Galilee. Salted and dried fish constituted a local industry.

LIZARD (Lev. 11:30). Palestine has some forty species of lizard, including the green lizard, wall-lizard, sand lizard, monitor lizard and gecko (see also **CHAMELEON**).

PYTHONIC SPIRIT (SPIRIT OF DIVINATION), a form of oracular ventriloquism associated with the python overcome by Apollo at Delphi (Acts 16:16).

SERPENT (Gen. 3:1). Palestine has some eighteen species of snake. The fiery serpent (**saraph**) is mentioned in Num. 21:8 and Isa. 14:29, in the latter reference described as flying, perhaps indicating a species of lizard. The term fiery is believed to relate to the inflammation caused by snakebite (see also **ADDER**).

TORTOISE (Lev. 11:29). Well known in Palestine, but the Biblical reference is to a species of lizard.

VIPER (Job 20:6; Matt. 3:7, see also **ADDER**).

WHALE (Gen. 1:21). Whales are found in both the Mediterranean and the Red Sea, but the Biblical terms relate to large sea creatures in general.

INSECTS AND SMALL CREATURES

In the warm climate of Bible lands the insect world has been a dominant form of life, providing a moral for the philosopher, an instrument of national punishment in the fulminations of the prophet, and in many instances a constant menace and inconvenience represented demonically by Beelzebub (Lord of Flies). Many varieties were known which are not mentioned specifically in the Bible. This also applies to rodents and other small creatures. Some insects were eaten (Lev. 11:21).

ANT (Prob. 6:6). Chiefly the small red ant, but also the large black ant, and other varieties.

BALD LOCUST (Lev. 11:22).

BAT (Lev. 11:19). Some seventeen varieties.

BEE (Deut. 1:14). The Hebrew word is **deborah,** name of the prophetess who judged Israel (Judg. 4:4).

BEETLE (Lev. 11:22). Known in Palestine as in Egypt the **Scarabaeus sacer** was a popular symbol of regeneration and resurrection. The Biblical reference is probably to a species of locust, but some authorities understand the cricket.

CANKERWORM (Joel 1:4). The larval state of the locust.

CATERPILLAR (I Kings 8:37). The **chasil** was a kind of locust, but of course the caterpillar was a common sight since there was an abundance of moths and butterflies.

CENTIPEDE (Lev. 11:5, "that which hath many feet").

CONEY (Lev. 11:5). Incorrect translation of the Hebrew **shaphan,** the creature being the **Hyrax syriacus** (rock badger).

CRICKET (see **BEETLE**).

FERRET (Lev. 11:30). Incorrect translation, possibly the gecko, but some understand the hedgehog.

FLEA (I Sam. 24:14).

FLY (Exod. 8:21; Ps. 78:45; Eccles. 10:1). In the first two references the Hebrew **arob** may mean the gadfly or the tsetse. The housefly, Hebrew **zebub,** is indicated in the third reference.

GNAT (Matt. 23:24). Some authorities understand the mosquito. In the Revised Standard Version a reference to gnats occurs in Isa. 51:6.

GRASSHOPPER (Lev. 11:22). The Hebrew **chagab** may mean a species of small locust. Other words which should be translated locust are **arbeh** (Judg. 6:5) and **gob** (Amos 7:1). It is not possible to make clear distinction between the various hopping insects.

HORNET (Exod. 23:28). The hornet or wasp.

HORSE-LEECH (Prov. 30:15). The leech was common in Palestine and used for medical treatment.

LOCUST (Exod. 10:4; Matt. 3:4). The locust was the scourge of the Middle East, as it still is. Several varieties and stages of growth are mentioned in the Bible and sometimes another insect is named in error (see also **GRASSHOPPER**). Dried locusts were an article of diet.

LOUSE (Exod. 8:16).

MOLE (Isa. 2:20). Probably the mole-rat. The word rendered mole in Lev. 11:30 refers to a species of lizard.

MOTH (Job 4:19; Matt. 6:19).

MOUSE (Lev. 11:29). The term covers various kinds of rodents, including dormice, field mice (I Sam. 6:4), and rats.

PALMERWORM (Joel 1:4). The locust at a stage in its growth.

RAT (see **MOUSE**).

SCORPION (Deut. 8:15; Luke 10:19). Member of the spider family with a sting in the end of its tail.

SNAIL (Ps. 58:8). The word translated snail in Lev. 11:30 refers to a species of lizard.

SPIDER (Job 8:14). The word translated spider in Prov. 30:28 refers to a species of lizard.

WEASEL (Lev. 11:29). Either the weasel or mole.

WORM (Mic. 7:17). Other biblical references such as Exod. 16:24 and Mark 9:44 are to kinds of maggots, while Isa. 51:8 refers to the moth grub or wood louse.

PLANTS AND TREES

The botanical references in the Bible have in many cases presented a serious problem of identification. Some are still doubtful or impossible to determine. Plants and herbs were greatly prized for their aromatic and medicinal properties, and were employed for seasoning. Flowers were appreciated, but few are named. While there were a number of forests and plantations, timber had largely to be imported. Fruit and grain provided the staple diet of the people and essential products like oil and wine ministered to their needs. Tree worship was widely practiced in Bible times. Among those held sacred were the oak, terebinth and date palm, and we find a Tree of Life and a Tree of Knowledge in the Garden of Eden. The story of the Trees who chose a King must be one of the oldest fables in the world (Judg. 9).

ALGUM (ALMUG) TREES (I Kings 10:11–12; II Chron. 2:8). Timber imported by King Solomon from Lebanon and Ophir, possibly red sandalwood.

ALMOND (Gen. 43:11). Called "the hastening tree" because the blossom comes before the leaves (Jer. 1:11–12).

ALOE, LIGN-ALOE (Num. 24:6; John 19:39). Used as a spice ingredient.

ANISE (Matt. 28:23). The reference is to dill.

APPLE (Prov. 25:11). The Biblical references are to the apricot or the quince.

APPLE OF SODOM, or Dead Sea Fruit. Fair without, but hollow within. Grows near the Dead Sea and may be alluded to in Deut. 32:32.

APRICOT (see **APPLE**).

ASH (Isa. 44:14). Probably the Aleppo pine.

BALM (Gen. 37:25). Probably mastic.

BARLEY (Exod. 9:7; Rev. 6:6). A staple food. First grain harvested in early Spring.

BAY TREE (Ps. 37:35).

BEANS (II Sam. 17:28). The broad bean.

BITTER HERBS (Exod. 12:8). Obligatory to be eaten at the Passover, and represented by chicory, endive, lettuce, watercress, and horseradish tops.

BOX TREE (Isa. 41:19).

BRAMBLE, BRIAR (Judg. 9:14; Mark 12:26). Five varieties of prickly shrub are mentioned in the Bible, which cannot be identified exactly, but would include cacti. (See also **THISTLE, THORN**).

BULRUSH (Isa. 58:5). (See also **REEDS**).

BURNING BUSH (Exod. 3:2). Believed to be the small acacia.

CALAMUS, SWEET CANE (Exod. 30:23; Isa. 43:24). Used in preparation of the sacred anointing oil.

CAMPHIRE (Song of Sol. 1:14). The reference is to henna.

CASSIA (Exod. 30:24). Used in making the sacred anointing oil, derived from the bark of a species of cinnamon tree.

CEDAR (Lev. 14:4). The reference here is to juniper.

CEDAR OF LEBANON (I Kings 4:33).

CHESTNUT (Gen. 30:37). The plane tree.

CINNAMON (Exod. 30:23).

CITRON. This is understood in Lev. 23:40. Used in the celebration of the Feast of Tabernacles.

COCKLE (Job 31:40). Some kind of noxious weed.

CORIANDER (Exod. 16:31). Seed used as flavoring, similar to caraway.

CORN (Gen. 41:40; Matt. 12:1). Various kinds of cereals including barley, wheat, and millet.

CUCUMBER (Num. 11:5).

CUMIN (Matt. 23:23).

CYPRESS TREE (Isa. 44:14), including the holm and ilex.

ELM (Hos. 4:13). The terebinth or poplar.

FIG (Gen. 3:7).

FIR TREE (II Kings 19:23). Various kinds of conifer come under this name.

FITCHES (i.e., **VETCHES**). Should be translated cumin in Isa. 28:25, and spelled in Ezek. 4:9.

FLAG (Exod. 2:3; Job 8:11). (See **REEDS**).

FLAX (Exod. 9:31; Matt. 12:20). Fiber of stalk is woven into linen.

FRANKINCENSE (Exod. 30:34; Matt 2:11). An aromatic gum resin.

GALBANUM (Exod. 30:34). Aromatic resin used in the making of incense.

GARLIC (Num. 11:5).

GOPHER WOOD (Gen. 6:14). Identification uncertain, employed in building Noah's Ark.

GOURD (Jonah 4:6–9). The bottle gourd, a rapid climber.

GOURD, WILD (II Kings 4:39). Identification uncertain.

GRAPE (see **VINE**).

GRASS, HAY (Gen. 1:11; Matt. 6:30). The term grass in the Bible covers all herbage on which cattle might graze, and different words distinguish its state rather than species.

GROVE (Gen. 21:33). Here meaning a tamarisk.

HAZEL (Gen. 30:37). The reference is to a nut-bearing tree, probably the almond.

HEATH (Jer. 17:6). The Hebrew word has the significance of bareness. Some authorities propose the dwarf juniper.

HEMLOCK, WORMWOOD (Deut. 29:18; Rev. 8:11). Some kind of plant with a bitter taste.

HENNA (see **CAMPHIRE**).

HYSSOP (Exod. 12:22; Heb. 9:19).

JUNIPER (I Kings 19:4). Probably a species of broom. (See also **CEDAR**).

LEEK (Num. 11:5).

LENTIL (Gen. 25:34).

LILY (Song of Sol. 2:1; Matt. 6:28). Either the anemone or wild iris.

MALLOW (Job 30:4).

MANDRAKE (or **LOVE APPLE**) believed to promote sexual fertility (Gen. 30:14).

MELON (Num. 11:5).

MILLET (Ezek. 4:9). Species of grain.

MINT (Matt. 23:23).

MULBERRY (II Sam. 5:23).

MUSTARD (Matt. 13:31).

MYRRH (Exod. 30:23; Matt. 2:11). An aromatic resin from certain shrubs. Another kind is referred to in Gen. 37:25.

MYRTLE TREE (Neh. 8:15).

NETTLE (Job 30:7). The stinging nettle. Another word translated nettle in Isa. 34:13 is probably the acanthus thorn.

NUT. Two Hebrew words. In Gen. 43:11 the pistachio nut, and in Song of Sol. 6:11 the walnut.

OAK (Gen. 35:8). Various species of oak are represented and also the terebinth (see **TEIL TREE**).

OIL TREE (I Kings 6:23). The oleaster.

OLIVE TREE (Gen. 8:11; Rom. 11:27).

ONION (Num. 11:5).

PALM TREE (Exod. 15:27; John 12:13). Particularly the date palm.

PAPER REEDS, PAPYRUS (Isa. 19:7). (See also **REEDS**).

PINE TREE (Isa. 41:10). The plane tree.

POMEGRANATE (Exod. 28:33).

POPLAR TREE (Hos. 4:13). The green poplar in Gen. 30:37 is believed to be the storax.

REEDS, RUSHES (Isa. 9:14; Jer. 51:32; I Kings 14:15; Matt. 11:7). Various kinds of reed, rush and cane growing in swampy areas.

ROSE, ROSE OF SHARON (Song of Sol. 2:1). The damask rose was sacred to Adonis in northern Palestine and Syria, but the rose of the Bible is the meadow saffron or crocus.

SAFFRON (Song of Sol. 4:14).

SHITTAH TREE, SHITTIM WOOD (Exod. 25:5). The gum arabic tree (**Acacia seyal**).

SPIKENARD (Song of Sol. 1:12; Mark 14:3). A kind of resinous gum is referred to as **SPICERY** (Gen. 37:25).

STACTE (Exod. 30:34). An aromatic gum.

SYCAMINE TREE (Luke 17:6). Probably the black mulberry.

SYCAMORE TREE (I Kings 10:27; Luke 19:4). The sycamore fig tree.

TARES (Matt. 13:24). Bearded darnel, a corn-like weed.

TEIL TREE (Isa. 6:13). The terebinth.

THISTLE, THORN (Gen. 3:18; II Kings 14:9; Matt. 7:16). Many varieties.

THYME (THYINE) WOOD (Rev. 18:12). Resembling the cypress.

VINE (Gen. 40:9; Matt. 26:29). The grape vine. The grapes provided fresh and dried fruit (raisins) and various types of wine.

WHEAT (Gen. 30:14; Matt. 3:12). Varieties including corn and millet.

WILLOW (Lev. 23:40; Ezek. 27:5). Two Hebrew words.

The first reference is to willows of the brook, probably the oleander, while the second is the willow tree.

WORMWOOD (see **HEMLOCK**).

WILD ANIMALS

Many wild animals mentioned in the Bible have long since become extinct in Palestine and neighboring lands. Identification is not in all cases certain, and several references in the King James Version are misleading.

ANTELOPE (see **BULL (OX), WILD**).

APE (I Kings 10:22). (See also **Domesticated Animals**).

ASS, WILD (Job 6:5, 39:5).

BADGER SKIN (Exod. 26:14). The skin of the seal or dugong.

BAT (Lev. 11:19). Listed in the Bible among winged creatures.

BEAR (I Sam. 17:34; Rev. 13:2). The Syrian bear.

BEHEMOTH (Job 40:15). The hippopotamus.

BOAR (Ps. 80:13). The wild boar.

BULL (OX), WILD (Deut. 14:5; Isa. 51:20). The sable antelope.

CHAMOIS (Deut. 14:5). Possibly the wild sheep.

DROMEDARY (see **Domesticated Animals**).

ELEPHANT (see **Domesticated Animals**).

FALLOW DEER (Deut. 14:5). Probably the roebuck or gazelle.

FOX (see **JACKAL**).

GAZELLE (Acts 9:36). Dorcas (Aram. **Tabitha**), name of a widow.

GOAT, WILD (Deut. 14:5). The ibex.

HARE (Lev. 11:6). Believed to be the hare-like **Lepus syriacus.**

HART, HIND (Deut. 12:15). Probably the red deer.

HIPPOPOTAMUS (see **BEHEMOTH**).

HYENA. Not mentioned by name in the Old Testament, but "speckled bird" Jer. 12:9 should probably be rendered hyena.

JACKAL and **FOX** (Judg. 15:4; Matt. 8:29). Only the fox is named, though jackal would in most cases be more correct. Both animals were well known.

LEOPARD (Song of Sol. 4:8; Rev. 13:2).

LION (Gen. 49:9; II Tim. 4:17).

PYGARG (Deut. 14:5). A member of the deer family, possibly the addax with twisted horns.

ROE, ROEBUCK (Deut. 12:15). A species of antelope.

UNICORN (Num. 23:22). The two-horned aurochs (wild ox) now extinct.

WOLF (Gen. 49:27; Matt. 7:15).

PART III

PEOPLES AND PLACES

According to the Bible (Gen. 10; I Chron. 1), the peoples of the ancient world derived from the descendants of the sons of Noah: Shem, Ham, and Japheth. The riddle of some of the names in the biblical lists has not yet been solved, and archaeological discoveries may yet throw further light on them. The Fertile Crescent was the scene of the history of many nations and tribes, those which developed great civilizations and are well known or comparatively so, and others obscure or of less significance. The interesting thing is that some influential peoples and cultures, which were hardly more than names not so long ago, have had to be given a much higher place in our estimation as a result of what we are learning about them. A few have been rescued from complete oblivion, thanks to the spades of the excavators. The scale of values has continually to be revised as more information about the remote past is obtained.

In determining which peoples should be mentioned, consideration has been paid to prominence in the Bible story, which includes the inter-testamental period, and also to importance for an understanding of the history of Bible lands. Those which have been largely passed over, though receiving incidental mention, are ones connected with city-states rather than with countries. Such were numerous in ancient times, and in many cases the cities concerned appear in the description of places in the second section of this Part. Their peoples constituted elements of various races and nations which are otherwise dealt with in the list. Again the qualification has to be made that in some cases there is not complete agreement among scholars.

The places are not confined to those which occur in the Bible, and choice has been governed not by size (town, village or building) but by consequence either in the Bible or in related history. Places which are more associated with natural features than with habitation have been covered in Part I, PHYSICAL GEOGRAPHY.

PEOPLES

ACHAEANS. This people, also known as Mycenaeans, from the center of their culture discovered by Schliemann at Mycenae, moved into Greece early in the 2nd millennium B.C. In due course they became strong enough to contend successfully with the Minoans of Crete for supremacy in the Aegean Sea. Around 1200 B.C. they were dispossessed by the barbarous Dorians, and sought new homes on the mainland of Asia Minor. Sweeping down the eastern Mediterranean in migratory waves, they reached and were turned back from Egypt, particularly by the victories of Rameses III. They were able to establish themselves, however, on the coasts of Phoenicia and Palestine about the same time as the Israelites from the east were securing their position in Canaan. A seagoing race, they were prominent in mercantile adventures. (See also **PEOPLES OF THE SEA, PHILISTINES,** and **PHOENICIANS**).

AKKADIANS. A semitic people who occupied northern Babylonia early in the 3rd millennium B.C., defeating the non-semitic Sumerians, but adopting much of their culture and the cuneiform style of writing. Early literary remains, like the Gilgamesh Epic, were translated into Akkadian, which was perpetuated as an official language down to the time of the Assyrian Empire. The founding of Akkad is attributed in the Bible to Nimrod (Gen. 10:10, but the dynasty of Akkad was established by Sargon I of Akkad (Agade), c.

2600 B.C. About 500 years later Sumer and Akkad were overrun by the Amorites.

AMALEKITES. Ancient nomadic people roving southern Palestine and the Sinai peninsula. The Amalekites opposed the Israelites on their journey from Egypt and were defeated by Joshua at the battle of Rephidim (Exod. 17). Perpetual war was decreed against them. The conflict had its climax in the reigns of Saul (I Sam. 15) and David (II Sam. 8), but tribes of Amalekites still existed in the time of King Hezekiah 300 years later (I Chron. 4:43).

AMMONITES. People of Transjordan contemporary with the history of Israel, having their capital at Rabbat-Ammon (now Amman, capital of Jordan). In Gen. 19:38 their origin is traced to Lot, nephew of Abraham. They were frequently in conflict with Israel and Judah, but there were also close relations and intermarriages.

AMORITES. A powerful semitic people divided into a number of branches whose original home was northeast of Mesopotamia. In the 3rd millennium B.C. they established the flourishing and progressive kingdom of Mari on the upper Euphrates, which for centuries controlled the east-west trade route. The Amorites invaded southern Mesopotamia, overcoming the Sumerians and Akkadians, and created the first Babylonian Empire. The great Amorite king Hammurabi was the sixth monarch of the 1st dynasty of Babylon. Extending his conquests he destroyed the kingdom of Mari about 1700 B.C. The family to which the patriarch Abraham belonged was settled in this kingdom, in the cities of Haran and Nahor. The Amorite and Hittite associations of the Hebrew race are mentioned in Ezek. 16:3. Later, the Amorite homeland was overrun from the north by the Hurrians and Hittites, and at the time of the Israelite advance to Canaan the Amorites were in command of the mountainous country east of the Jordan. Under their king Sihon, whose capital was at Heshbon, they opposed Israel and were defeated (Num. 21). The fertility cult of the Amorites, like that of the Moabites, was a continual menace to the purity of Hebrew worship.

ARABIANS. In early biblical history they are nomadic tribes of the eastern desert, largely semitic, dwelling in tents. With southern Arabians the Israelites had little to do until the time of Solomon. The Arabians of the south and east of Palestine were more strongly organized in later Jewish history, playing a part in the power struggles of the region with capitals at Damascus and Petra. (See also **NABATAEANS**).

ARAMAEANS. A semitic people related to the Amorites (the Tigris-Euphrates area is called in the Bible Aram-Naharaim, Aram of the Two Rivers). From the Aramaeans in the east came the Chaldaeans, who created the revived Babylonian Empire of the 7th century B.C. (the Mesopotamian city from which Abraham came appears in the Bible as Ur of the Chaldees). In the west they were well-established in northern Palestine in the 2nd millennium B.C., and became prominent towards 1000 B.C. in the group of kingdoms constituting Aram, translated Syria in the King James Version. They presented a serious threat to Assyria, and were sometimes allies and sometimes foes of Israel. Their language, Aramaic, was in widespread use, and in the post-exilic period its written characters (the square characters) were borrowed by the Jews for Hebrew in substitution for the Phoenician script of the earlier period. A dialect of Aramaic was spoken by Jesus. The western Aramaean area became Coele-Syria in Greco-Roman times, and flourished in the 3rd century B.C. under the Seleucid monarchs, with capital at Antioch on the Orontes. Ultimately Syria became a province of the Roman Empire.

ASSYRIANS. A semitic people who had their homeland in a region anciently called Subartu, later Ashur, on the upper Tigris. On the west their territory bordered that of Mari. Their early history can now be traced fairly clearly; but it is from the 14th to the 7th century B.C. that they played an important part in affairs with which the Bible is concerned, this period representing the rise and fall of the Assyrian Empire. In Gen. 10 reference is made to the beginning of this power with respect to its great cities, of which Nineveh became the chief. By the time of Solomon, king of Israel, the Assyrians were carving out a great empire, going forth conquering and to conquer with much cruelty. They destroyed the kingdom of Israel and almost overcame Judah in the days of Hezekiah (II Kings and Isaiah). Finally, however, Assyria was crushed by combined forces of Babylonians, Medes, and Scythians, and Nineveh was sacked in 612 B.C. (Nah. 3:1–3).

BABYLONIANS. The Babylonians were a blend of semitic (Akkadian and Amorite) and non-semitic (Sumerian and Kassite) stock, with the semitic predominating. They therefore had much in common with the Assyrians in their religion, culture and way of life. The first Babylonian Empire had been Amoritic; the second was Chaldean, and had a brief burst of glory under Nabopolasser and Nebuchadnezzar. Only a few years after the death of the latter, when Nabonidus was king and his son Belshazzar was regent, Babylon fell to the Medo-Persians under Cyrus in 539 B.C. In the Bible this period is well-represented in the books of Kings and Chronicles and Ezra-Nehemiah and the prophets Isaiah, Jeremiah, Ezekiel, Haggai and Zechariah, because of the Babylonian exile and the return. Jewish religious thought was considerably affected by Babylonian influences.

CANAANITES. The Canaanites of the Bible represent a mixture of races and peoples largely semitic, but not exclusively so, settled primarily in various city-states of the coastal region of the east Mediterranean. The name may mean Lowlanders, or perhaps Red from a Hurrian word, which the Greeks converted into Phoenician. As an agricultural people fertility rites were prominent in their religion. El was the chief god-name among them, with each center having its Baal, or spiritual lord (Adon), and sovereign lady Ashtoreth-Astarte (Ishtar), Queen of Heaven. In later times, because of their commercial activities, the name Canaanite came to have the signification of merchant (Isa. 23:8). (See also **PHOENICIANS**).

CHALDAEANS (see **ARAMAEANS**).

CRETANS. People of the island of Crete, whose highest culture was achieved under the Minoan civilization of the 2nd millennium B.C. with the capital at Knossos. The Minoans were in command of the Aegean until challenged and finally defeated by the Achaeans, and Crete became part of the Hellenic world. It is not certain that Caphtor, ancestral home of the Philistines (Jer. 47:4; Amos 9:7), represents Crete: an association has been proposed with the part of Asia Minor later called Cappadocia. But Cretans of Achaean stock like the Philistines were enrolled in David's bodyguard (Cherethites and Pelethites, II Sam. 8:18), having settled in Philistia. (See also **PEOPLES OF THE SEA**).

CUSHITES (see **ETHIOPIANS**).

CUTHITES (see **SAMARITANS**).

CYPRIOTS (see **KITTIM**).

EDOMITES. A people living largely like bedouin, inhabiting an area in the region of Mt. Seir southwest of the Dead Sea. In the Bible they are an offshoot of the Hebrews, deriving from Esau, brother of Jacob and grandson of Abraham (Gen. 36:9); and the Edomites are described as brothers of the Israelites (Deut. 23:7). Yet there was war and frequent conflict between them. In the time of the Maccabees the land of the Edomites had become Idumea, and the people were forcibly converted to Judaism under John Hyrcanus I. An Idumean, Herod the Great, became king of the Jews.

EGYPTIANS. The ancient people of the Nile Valley of hamitic African stock who gave rise to one of the greatest of the early civilizations. Their country was organized as kingdoms of Upper and Lower Egypt (hence the dual form of the Hebrew name for Egypt **Mitsraim**) under a succession of kings known as the Pharaoh, listed in dynasties (30 according to the Egyptian historian Manetho). From Patriarchal times the Egyptians were more closely connected with Biblical history than any other people. The story of the Israelites as a nation begins in Egypt where they were a subject people. For centuries before the Exodus, and for some time after, the Egyptians were overlords of Palestine, though earlier in the 2nd millennium Egypt had been ruled by mainly semitic northern invaders (see under **HYKSOS**). This period had coincided with that of the Hebrew Patriarchs. Egyptian power was in decline when Assyria and Babylonia were in the ascendant, and Egypt came successively under the control of Persia, Greece and Rome; but it continued to be a great spiritual and intellectual center.

ELAMITES. A people having their homeland east of Babylonia with their capital at Susa. Their pressure upon Mesopotamia at different epochs strongly affected the history of the Land of the Two Rivers, especially from the 12th to the 7th century B.C. The prophetic books of the Bible have a number of references to them (e.g., Isa. 11:2; Jer. 49:34–39; Ezek. 32:24). In the battle of the four kings with five in the time of Abraham (Gen. 14) the king of Elam (Chedorlaomer) appears as the head of the eastern confederacy.

ETHIOPIANS. The Ethiopians of the Bible, of dark-skinned hamitic stock, inhabited the area on the southern borders of Egypt known as Cush (eastern Sudan and part of what is now Ethiopia) and subsequently Nubia. The Ethiopian treasurer of Queen Candace (Acts 8) was a Nubian. The later rulers of Ethiopia claimed descent from a son born to Solomon and the Queen of Sheba. Nubian culture was linked with that of Egypt.

GALATIANS. An Indo-European people settled in central Asia Minor south of the Black Sea about 300 B.C. Their country was made a Roman Province. They were evangelized by St. Paul.

GREEKS, HELLENES (Hebrew **Javanim** = Ionians). The Javanim were the peoples occupying the Greek mainland and archipelago, consisting of various migrating tribes, Achaeans, Dorians, Pelasgians, Spartans, etc. Greek civilization did not materially affect Jewish life and thought until about the 4th century B.C., and its impact came largely through the Macedonians, with the conquests of Alexander the Great, and increased under the Seleucids and Ptolemies. The attempt made early in the 2nd century B.C. to substitute Greek worship for Judaism was resisted and defeated by the Maccabees and their supporters. St. Paul preached in Greece (Macedonia and Achaia) and founded a number of churches, but made little headway at Athens.

HEBREWS. People whose original homeland is believed to have been southern Arabia. Some of their clans migrated to Mesopotamia, and from one of them sprang Abram (Abraham) the Hebrew. There were pockets of them in the north in the area ruled by Mari early in the 2nd millennium B.C., and some like Abraham followed the Fertile Crescent into Canaan. These semi-nomadic clans are probably to be identified with the Mesopotamian Habiru and the Egyptian 'Apiru. (See also **ISRAELITES**).

HITTITES. A powerful people of Indo-European origin who made their way into Asia Minor about 2000 B.C., overrunning and absorbing the Hatti, and so becoming known as the Hittites (Egyptian, Kheta). Their empire, with capital at Hattushash, largely controlled Asia Minor from about 1400-1200 B.C., and settlements of theirs were to be found far to the south, where Abraham bought from them the Cave of Machpelah (Gen. 23). The Hittites had their own language and religion and were a cultured and humane people. Colonies of Hittites were to be found in Syria and Palestine long after the disintegration of their empire.

HURRIANS (HORITES). An Armenoid Caucasian people who spread to the south and west from the area of Lake Van around the beginning of the 2nd millennium B.C., controlling especially the kingdom of Mitanni and having contact with the early Hebrews. Hittite expansion incorporated the Hurrians; but like the Hebrews, elements of the Hurrians had moved round the Fertile Crescent into Palestine and had established settlements in various parts of the country, notably in the Edomite area. They are called Horites in the Bible, and were known to the Egyptians as Hurru.

HYKSOS. Not strictly a people, but confederate "chieftains" of mixed peoples, mainly semitic like the Amorites, who swept down into Egypt in the 18th century B.C. and ruled the country for nearly 200 years with their capital at Avaris. Hyksos control of Egypt covered the period of Joseph, who rose to high office under one of their Pharaohs, and the settlement of the Israelites in Goshen.

IDUMEANS (see **EDOMITES**).

ISRAELITES. The branch of the Hebrews deriving from the descendants of the children of the patriarch Jacob (called Israel). Led out from Egypt by Moses, and welded into a nation in the wilderness, they conquered much of Canaan under Joshua and his successors, and were formed into a kingdom which developed in the reigns of Saul, David and Solomon. Under the latter the foundations of an empire were laid, which did not materialize. In the reign of Solomon's son Rehoboam the kingdom was divided. The northern kingdom, known as Israel, lasted until overthrown by the Assyrians in 722 B.C. The southern kingdom, known as Judah, lasted a further century and a half until destroyed by the Babylonians in 586 B.C. Elements of Israel had become integrated with the Judeans (Jews), and the Jewish people perpetuated the name of Israelites. They cherished an expectation that the descendants of the exiled Israelites would ultimately return and be reunited with their brethren in an ideal kingdom representative of all Israel. (See also **SAMARITANS**).

JAVANIM (see **GREEKS**).

JEWS (see **ISRAELITES**).

KASSITES. A barbarian people from the region of the Zagros mountains who occupied Babylon from about 1500 to 1100 B.C. Coming from the northeast of Mesopotamia they were able to take advantage of the vacuum left by the Hittites, who having conquered Babylon subsequently abandoned it. Kassite relations with Egypt enter into the correspondence recorded in the Tell el-Amarna tablets.

KENITES (see **MIDIANITES**).

KITTIM. The people of Cyprus, particularly Phoenician (Isa. 23:1). Under the Seleucid kings who ruled Syria in the 3rd and 2nd century B.C. the Jews called the Macedonians Kittim, and the name was applied to the Romans when they controlled the Near East. Many Jews were settled in Cyprus and the Apostle Barnabas was a Cypriote.

LIBYANS. The Lubim of Nah. 3:9, people of the coastal region west of Egypt who were frequently in conflict with the Egyptians. In New Testament times many Jews were settled in cities here, especially Cyrene (Matt. 27:32; Acts 2:10, 11:20).

MACEDONIANS. A wild people of northern Greece, who adopted the Hellenic language and culture. They came to prominence in the 4th century under Philip II of Macedon and his son Alexander the Great, who overthrew the Persian Empire and created a vast but short-lived one of his own. The Jews threw in their lot with the Macedonians.

MEDES. An Indo-European people who effectively established themselves northeast of Assyria early in the 1st millennium B.C., and under their king Cyaxares combined with Babylonians and Scythians to conquer Assyria between 616 and 612 B.C. In the reign of Cyrus (550-529 B.C.) the Medo-Persian Empire was established and extended east and west by his successors Cambyses and Darius I, until it embraced a vast area from the Nile to the Indus. The Medes were an enlightened and very cultured people. (See also **PERSIANS**).

MIDIANITES. A nomadic people centered in the region of the Gulf of 'Aqaba. Midianite traders carried Joseph son of Jacob to Egypt as a slave (Gen. 37), and Moses took refuge with them, marrying the daughter of the priest of Midian, Jethro, also called Ruel (Exod. 2). Hostilities between the Israelites and Midianites are described in Num.

31 and Judg. 6. A tribe of Midianites, the Kenites, was protected by Israel (I Sam 15:6).

MINOANS (see **CRETANS**).

MOABITES. A semitic people of the region immediately east of the Dead Sea. Their history was closely associated with that of the Israelites with whom they were frequently in conflict. Balak, king of Moab, brought Balaam to curse Israel (Num. 22), but Ruth the Moabitess was an ancestor of King David. From the period of the kings of Israel and Judah has come the important inscription of Mesha king of Moab (Moabite Stone) telling of his recapture of various places from Ahab king of Israel.

MYCENAEANS (see **ACHAEANS**).

NABATAEANS. An Arab people with capital at Petra with whom the Jews had good relations in the period of the Hasmoneans and Herodians. Several of their kings with the dynastic name of Haretath (Aretas) enter into Jewish history. Aretas IV was father-in-law to Herod Antipas, and attempted to seize St. Paul at Damascus (II Cor. 11:32).

NUBIANS (see **ETHIOPIANS**).

PARTHIANS. A powerful Iranian people east of the Euphrates who in the 2nd century B.C. under their king Mithradates the Great, succeeded in partially restoring the Medo-Persian Empire. The Parthian Empire impinged upon the eastern Provinces of the Roman Empire, and the two were in continual conflict. A revolt of the Persians put an end to the Parthian Empire in the 3rd century A.D. The Parthians were a warlike rather than a cultured people, but they were friendly to the Jews, many of whom were their subjects (Acts 2:9). The Jews hoped that Parthian intervention would destroy the Roman Empire, and this belief finds an echo in Rev. 16:12.

PEOPLES OF THE SEA. From Egyptian records we learn of sea-borne migrations of mixed peoples from the Aegean, among them the Philistines, who descended on the coasts of Canaan and attempted to invade Egypt. This movement coincided with the period of the Judges in Israel. The "Peoples of the Sea" were defeated by Rameses III in a great naval battle c.1190 B.C.

PERSIANS. An Indo-European people who with the

Medes established a great and opulent empire in the 6th century B.C. Cyrus, conqueror of Babylon, permitted the return of the Jewish exiles to Judea and the rebuilding of the Temple at Jerusalem. The Jews remained under Persian rule until that empire was overthrown by Alexander the Great. Previously the Persians had been defeated by the Greeks. The Persians followed the Magian faith reformed by the sage Zarathustra (Zoroaster), and their religion exercised a considerable influence on the development of Judaism. They made a great contribution to the arts, and the palace of the Great King at Persepolis was a marvel of beauty.

PHILISTINES. A people whose origin is not certain and who came from a region called Caphtor in the Bible. They appear under their name of Philistines (Hebrew **Pelishtim,** Egyptian, **Peleset**) among the "Peoples of the Sea" who settled on the southern coast of Canaan in the 12th century B.C. and for some 150 years fought fiercely with the Israelites. The Hebrew hero of the struggle was Samson (Judg. 13–16). The Philistines were often victorious: they even captured the Ark of the Covenant and prohibited the Israelites from having iron weapons. David killed their champion Goliath and finally subdued them. The Philistine government was in the hands of the lords of a confederacy of five city-states. From Philistia comes the general name Palestine.

PHOENICIANS. The Phoenicians were the product of the mingling of Canaanites and Achaeans, with the semitic element predominating. Occupying a coastal strip of the Mediterranean, largely corresponding to modern Lebanon, they were organized in city-states, notably at Tyre, Sidon, Gebal (Byblos), Berut (Beirut) and Ugarit (Ras Shamra). The Phoenicians, inevitably, were seafaring people with a mercantile marine trading in distant waters as far as Britain; and they established colonies in North Africa and Spain. Carthage in North Africa eventually challenged the might of Rome. The great period of Phoenician history was approximately from 1150-850 B.C. In this period there were close connections between Phoenicia and Israel. Hiram, king of Tyre, was allied to Solomon, king of Israel, and furnished materials and craftsmen for building the Temple at Jerusalem. Ahab, king of Israel, married Jezebel, daughter of Ithobaal, king of Sidon. Shortly before the time of Solomon we have the Egyptian account of the mission of Wen-Amum to obtain cedar wood from Zakarbaal, king of Byblos. To Phoenicia the West owes its alphabet, and from Byblos comes our word Bible.

ROMANS. A Latin race strongly influenced by Etruscan culture, whose development dates from the 8th century B.C. Rome was founded c.753. The Romans became allied with the Jews in the 2nd century B.C., and intervened directly in Jewish affairs from the time of Pompey (63 B.C.). Herod the Great owed his throne to Antony and Octavian (afterwards the Emperor Augustus), and after the deposition of his son Archelaus in 6 A.D., except for the brief reign of Agrippa I (41-44), the Romans governed Judea through procurators until the Jewish revolt and war with the Romans began in 66 A.D. With the destruction of Carthage in the last Punic War (146 B.C.) the Romans became the greatest power in the western world, and their empire, expanded to cover most of Europe and the Near East, was dominant in New Testament times. By their discipline and talent for organization and intrigue they maintained a hold over subject peoples, having created an effective fighting machine and systems of land and sea communications. Much of their culture, however, was borrowed from the Greeks. By the Romans the Christians were regarded as subversive and their religion was outlawed. Their regime was sustained by a cult of Rome and the Emperor.

SAMARITANS. They were known to the Jews as Cuthites because, according to the Bible (II Kings 17), they originated from peoples from Cuth and elsewhere whom the Assyrians had placed in the cities of Israel after the capture of Samaria in 722 B.C. They accepted the God of Israel, but continued much of their pagan worship. The Samaritans claimed, however, that they were the true Israel and that the Jews had falsified the Law and changed the appointed center of Divine worship from Mt. Gerizim at Shechem to Mt. Zion in Jerusalem. Their territory was called Samerinaa and later Samaria, occupying the center of Palestine. From the time of the Jewish return from Babylon there was strife with the Samaritans, who built their own temple on Mt. Gerizim and followed their own version of the Pentateuch. The conflict is represented in the Bible in the books of Ezra-Nehemiah and the Gospels. Additional information is to be found in the works of Josephus, Jewish historian of the 1st century A.D. The Samaritans have survived to the present day at Shechem (Nablus) and in Israel.

SUMERIANS. This people originally came as settlers to the rich lands of southern Mesopotamia, probably from further east (Gen. 11:2), their culture having an affinity with that of the Indus Valley. They called their new home Shumer (Sumer), the biblical Shinar, and they could trace their history back to before the flood. One of the Sumerian epics, that of Gilgamesh, includes an account of this event related by Utnapishtim, the Sumerian Noah. The dynasties of Sumarian rulers were associated with the chief cities, among them Erech, Nippur, Ur, Kish, and Lagash. Each city had its own presiding divinity, who was regarded as the real ruler. Sumerian history falls mainly within the period c.3000-2000 B.C., with an interruption of Akkadian domination. About 1950 B.C. Sumer, like Akkad, succumbed to the Amorites, who, however, adopted much of Sumerian culture. The Sumerians remarkably developed the art of government and the institutions of law. They kept excellent records, and the scribe was greatly honored among them. Their civilization continued to exercise an influence for many centuries after they had become merged with other peoples.

SYRIANS (see **ARAMAEANS**).

PLACES

AELIA CAPITOLINA (see **JERUSALEM**).

AI. Canaanite city near Bethel (Gen. 12:8) destroyed by Joshua (Josh. 7:8).

AKKAD (AGADE). City of the Akkadians in Mesopotamia. Its best-known ruler was Sargon I (c.2600 B.C.).

ALEXANDRIA (in Egypt). The great city founded by Alexander the Great in which many Jews were settled. Until the Roman annexation it was governed by the Ptolemaic dynasty. Its lighthouse (Pharos) was one of the wonders of the world, and it was famed for its library created by Ptolemy I and developed by Ptolemy II to whose encouragement is attributed the translation of the Pentateuch into Greek (Septuagint version). Alexandria became the chief center of Hellenic culture.

ANTIOCH (on the Orontes). Capital of the Seleucid dynasty in Syria. It was famed for its corso five miles long lined with statuary. Under the Romans it was the third metropolis of their empire and seat of the Roman legate superior of the governor of Judea. Here the disciples of Jesus were first called Christians (Acts 11:26), and from here St. Paul set out on his first missionary journey (Acts 11:26).

ANTIOCH (in Pisidia). Evangelized by St. Paul (Acts 13:14).

ANTONIA (fortress). It bore this name in New Testament times and overlooked the Temple area at Jerusalem. The ceremonial robes of the high priest were kept there by the Romans, who had a garrison in the fort to prevent rebellious outbreaks. Here St. Paul was brought for questioning (Acts. 21–22) and, some hold, Jesus was tried before Pilate. The site is now occupied by the Convent of the Sisters of Zion, and the paved court of the fortress has been uncovered in the crypt.

ASHDOD. One of the five cities of the Philistines. Here the captured Ark of the Covenant was brought (I Sam. 5:1). Under its later Greek name of Azotus it is mentioned in Acts 8:40.

ASHKELON (ASKELON). One of the Philistine cities.

ASSHUR (ASHUR). Ancient city on the Tigris, capital of the Assyrian Empire and cult-center of the Assyrian national deity of the same name.

ATHENS. Capital of Attic Greece, and under the Romans a city of the Province of Achaia. The Temple of Athene, the Parthenon, crowned the Acropolis hill. Nearby was Mars Hill (Areopagus) where St. Paul defended his beliefs (Acts 17). The market (**Agora**), where Paul also preached, was the meeting-place of the philosophical schools, the Epicureans and the Stoics (called after the colonnades, or **stoa**). At a shop in this market Socrates had taught.

AVARIS. Capital of Egypt during the Hyksos occupation. Identified with Tanis, the Zoan of the Bible (Isa. 19:11). It was rebuilt by Rameses II, probably the Pharaoh who oppressed the Israelites. Situated in the Delta on an eastern branch of the Nile, it was one of the chief cities of Lower Egypt.

AZOTUS (see **ASHDOD**).

BABEL (tower of). The building of it is described in Gen. 11. The great brick structure of pyramidal type (ziggurat) at Babylon, consisted of seven tiers or stages, with the Temple of Marduk, patron deity of Babylon, at the top. It rose to a height of approximately 300 feet. The Babylonians called it **Etemenanki** (house of the foundations of heaven and earth). It was said of it, very much like the account in the Bible, that it "lifted its pinnacle into the sky."

BABYLON. Capital of Babylonia from the 18th century B.C., situated on a canal dug from the Euphrates. It reached the height of its glory at the beginning of the 6th century B.C. under Nebuchadnezzar II, a great walled city with its splendid Ishtar Gate and famous hanging gardens, in addition to the Temple of Marduk. To Babylon was brought the Jewish king Jehoiachin and his family (II Kings 24:15), and Babylonian records show that he was well treated. Babylon fell to the Persians in 539 B.C. when Belshazzar was acting as regent for his father Nabonidus (Dan. 5).

BEERSHEBA. Town of the Negeb where there were wells. Abraham and his family made a home there (Gen. 22:9). For the Israelites it was the southern border of their country "Dan to Beersheba" (I Sam. 3:20).

BETHANY. Village on the east of the Mt. of Olives, home of Martha, Mary, and Lazarus, friends of Jesus.

BETHEL. Town formerly called Luz, scene of Jacob's vision (Gen. 28) and a center of worship under Jeroboam I (I Kings 12).

BETHLEHEM. Chiefly the city of David in Judah south

of Jerusalem, prophetically birthplace of the Messiah (Matt. 2).

BETHSAIDA. Fishing village on the Lake of Galilee, home of Andrew and Peter and Philip (John 1). Another Bethsaida northeast of the lake was rebuilt by Philip the tetrarch and called Julias, scene of the feeding of the 5000 (Luke 9).

BETHSHEAN (BETHSHAN). Canaanite city of the Valley of Jezreel, where Saul's body was placed by the Philistines after the battle of Mt. Gilboa (I Sam. 31). In the Hellenic period called Scythopolis, one of the 10 Greek cities forming the Decapolis (Matt. 4:35).

BETHSHEMESH. Where the Ark of the Covenant was brought when returned by the Philistines (I Sam. 6).

BYBLOS. The Phoenician city of Gebel (Ezek. 27:9), north of Beirut.

CAESAREA. Seaport on the coast of Palestine built by Herod the Great, at a place formerly called Strato's Tower. It figured prominently in Jewish history under the Romans and was the place of residence of the governor. The centurion Cornelius of Caesarea became a Christian (Acts 10) and St. Paul was imprisoned there (Acts 23–25).

CAESAREA-PHILIPPI. City at the source of the Jordan, otherwise called Paneas (from the nearby sanctuary of the god Pan). Jesus came as far north as this region (Mark 8:27).

CALAH. Ancient city on the Tigris south of Nineveh (Gen. 10:11), which in later times was the official residence of the kings of Assyria. The site now called Nimrud was one of the first of the Assyrian cities to be excavated, and here was found the famous Black Obelisk of Shalmaneser III which includes a record of the tribute paid by Jehu king of Israel.

CANA. Town of Galilee where Jesus performed a miracle (John 2).

CAPERNAUM. Town on the western shore of the Lake of Galilee where Jesus made his home and taught (Matt. 4:13). An ancient synagogue found here may have stood on the site of the one in which Jesus worshiped.

CARCHEMISH. A capital city of the Hittites on the

Euphrates in northern Syria, scene of a famous battle between the Egyptians and Assyrians (II Chron. 35:20).

CARTHAGE. City on the coast of North Africa near modern Tunis founded by the Phoenicians c.814 B.C. It became the capital of a Phoenician state able to challenge the might of Rome under the famous Hannibal. Carthage was destroyed by the Romans in 145 B.C. at the end of the long drawn-out struggle of the three Punic wars.

COLOSSAE. City of Phrygia on the river Lycus. St. Paul wrote the Epistle to the Colossians to the Christians there.

CORINTH. Greek port and capital city of the Roman Province of Achaia on the isthmus between the mainland and the Peloponnesus. It had a considerable Jewish population and St. Paul taught there for a year and a half (Acts 18) when Gallio, brother of Seneca, was proconsul of Achaia. To the Christian community St. Paul addressed the Epistles to the Corinthians.

DAMASCUS. A very ancient city of Syria near Mt. Hermon and close to the northern Arabian desert. Abraham's steward Eliezer came from Damascus (Genesis 15:2). The city achieved prominence as the Aramaean capital in the time of the kings of Israel and Judah, and later under Arab rulers. It became one of the cities of the Decapolis, and was the scene of St. Paul's conversion (Acts 9).

DERBE. City of Lycaonia evangelized with Lystra by St. Paul during his first missionary journey (Acts 14).

ECBATANA. Capital of Media. It figures in the Apocrypha especially in the story of Tobit.

EKRON. One of the five cities of the Philistines.

EMMAUS. Notably the village of this name near Jerusalem where Jesus appeared to two disciples after his resurrection (Luke 24).

EPHESUS. City of Asia Minor on the River Cayster and capital of the Roman Province of Asia. Famed for its Temple of Artemis (Diana) of which the chief benefactors had been King Croesus of Lydia and Alexander the Great. At Ephesus festivals and games were held in honor of the Roman emperors under the authority of Asiarchs. St. Paul taught in Ephesus (Acts 19) and wrote to the churches the letter known as the Epistle to the Ephesians.

ERECH. A very ancient city of southern Mesopotamia (Gen. 10:10) under the patronage of the sky-god Anu. It figures continually in Babylonian history.

EZION-GEBER. Near Elath on the Gulf of 'Aqaba. The Israelites halted here on their way from Egypt (Num. 33), and it was the home port of Solomon's fleet (I Kings 9:26).

FLAVIA NEAPOLIS (see **SHECHEM**).

GADARA. One of the cities of the Decapolis southeast of the Lake of Galilee. On the nearby shore the Gospel incident of the Gadarene swine took place (Mark 5).

GATH. One of the five cities of the Philistines, and home of their champion, Goliath, killed by David (I Sam. 17). Later, David took refuge with Achish king of Gath (I Sam. 27).

GAZA. One of the five cities of the Philistines, on the route to Egypt. Mentioned in Acts 8:26.

GEBAL (see **BYBLOS**).

GERASA. An important city of the Decapolis.

GIBEAH. The best known city of this name was in the territory of Benjamin, north of Jerusalem, the royal city of Saul, king of Israel (I Sam. 15:34).

GIBEON. City of Benjamin where there was a high place of worship. Solomon sacrificed there and in a dream was granted the gift of wisdom (I Kings 3:4–15).

GILGAL. Name of places where there was an ancient stone circle. The making of a gilgal representing the 12 tribes of Israel is attributed to Joshua (4:20) after the crossing of the River Jordan. This one, formerly a place of pagan worship, became an important Hebrew sanctuary where Saul was confirmed as king (I Sam. 11:8, 11:14).

GOMORRAH. One of the group of five city-states in the southern region of the Dead Sea. It is chiefly associated with one of them, Sodom, as a symbol of immorality. Destroyed in a natural disaster (Gen. 19:24).

HAMATH. On the River Orontes, an important city-state in Syria. The most northerly limit of the Promised Land (Num. 34:8).

HARAN. Town of northern Mesopotamia where Terah, father of Abraham, died (Gen. 11:32). From Haran Abraham journeyed to Canaan.

HATTUSHASH. Capital city of the great Hittite Empire. Near the modern Boghaz-keui, east of Ankara in Turkey.

HAZOR. Canaanite royal city north of the Lake of Galilee, chief of a league of city-states, destroyed by Joshua in the time of its king Jabin (Josh. 11). Rebuilt as a fortress by Solomon (I Kings 9:15).

HEBRON. Canaanite royal city called Kiriath-Arba (Gen. 23:2). Here Abraham dwelt and purchased the cave of Machpelah as a sepulcher for his wife Sarah. David was anointed king at Hebron (II Sam. 2:4).

HELIOPOLIS (see **ON**).

HESHBON. Capital city of Sihon, king of the Amorites, (Num. 30:26). Later a city of the Moabites. Fishpools there are mentioned in Song of Sol. 7:4.

HIPPICUS. Chief of three towers of the palace of Herod the Great at Jerusalem. The palace was later used by the Roman governors when they resided in the city, and it was probably the scene of the trial of Jesus.

ICONIUM. City of the Roman Province of Galatia, visited by St. Paul (Acts 13:51, 14:1).

ISIN. Ancient Sumerian city of southern Mesopotamia, and seat of a dynasty of kings from the 20th to the 18th century B.C.

JABNEEL (JAMNIA). Town of Palestine near the coast south of Joppa. The Jewish Sanhedrin reconstituted here after the destruction of the Temple in 70 A.D.

JEBUS (see **JERUSALEM**).

JERICHO. In the Jordan valley near the Dead Sea, center of an extremely ancient Stone Age civilization. The capture of Jericho by Joshua gave the Israelites the key to Canaan (Josh. 6). The Jericho of New Testament times, City of Palm Trees, lay south of the old city, and was a favorite resort of Herod the Great. Jesus passed through Jericho on his last journey to Jerusalem (Luke 18–19).

JERUSALEM. Melchizedek, who blessed Abraham, was priest-king of Salem (Gen. 14:18). The city was called Jebus when it was a Jebusite stronghold. It was captured by David (II Sam. 5) and became the royal city of the Judean kings. With the building of the Temple by Solomon it became also the Holy City, poetically known as Ariel and Zion. Jerusalem was destroyed by the Babylonians in 586 B.C., and by the Romans in 70 A.D. A Roman city, Aelia Capitolina, was built on the site by the Emperor Hadrian.

JOPPA. Mediterranean seaport of Palestine, associated with the story of Perseus and Andromeda. The prophet Jonah took ship here (Jonah 1:3). In the New Testament, St. Peter lodged at Joppa in the house of Simon the tanner (Acts 10). Scene of a naval battle during the Jewish war with Rome. Now called Jaffa.

KADESH. Important ancient Canaanite city on the Orontes in Syria. Scene of a decisive battle between the Egyptians and the Hittites.

KADESH-BARNEA. City of southern Palestine on the fringe of the Sinai wilderness at the junction of ancient trade routes. The Israelites spent some time here on their way to the Promised Land (Num. 20; Deut. 1).

KIR-HARESETH. Kir of Moab, a capital city of the Moabites in the time of the kings of Judah and Israel (II Kings 3:25).

KIRIATH-JEARIM. Also called Kiriath-Baal (Josh. 15:50). Where the Ark of the Covenant rested when it was returned by the Philistines (I Sam. 7).

KISH. A very ancient royal city of the Sumerians in the 3rd millennium B.C. situated southeast of Babylon. The dynasty of Kish ended when power was seized by Sargon I the Akkadian c.2600 B.C.

LACHISH. Canaanite royal city which became a key city of southern Judah. In the Assyrian invasion of Judah it was captured by Sennacherib (II Kings 18:13). Later its fortifications resisted the forces of the Babylonian Nebuchadnezzar (Jer. 34:7). Letters of the time of this last struggle have been found written on potsherds.

LAGASH. Ancient royal city of the Sumerians in southern Mesopotamia. Notable among its rulers of whom we have knowledge was Prince Gudea, end of 21st century B.C.

LAODICEA. City of Asia Minor close to Colossae (Col. 2). Recipient of one of the letters to the Seven Churches (Rev. 3:14).

LARSA. Ancient city-state of the Sumerians in southern Mesopotamia. The kings of Larsa were rivals of those of Isin further north. Under the Amorite king Hammurabi Larsa became part of Babylonia.

LOD (LYDDA). Southeast of Joppa on the fringe of the plain of Sharon. In the New Testament it is called Lydda, where St. Peter performed a cure (Acts 9:32). The Greek name was Diospolis. It was the seat of a Rabbinical Academy after the fall of Jerusalem.

LUZ (see **BETHEL**).

LYSTRA. City of Lycaonia in Asia Minor where St. Paul cured a lame man (Acts 14). Here lived Timotheus, whom Paul made his assistant (Acts 16:1).

MACHAERUS. Fortress on the east of the Dead Sea near the southern border of Peraea, used to protect the country from the Arabs in New Testament times. Herod Antipas had a palace there, and in the dungeon of the fortress John the Baptist was imprisoned and later executed.

MAGDALA. Fortified place on the western shore of the Lake of Galilee which gave its name to the district from which came Mary Magdalene (Mary of Magdala), a disciple of Jesus (Luke 8:2).

MAHANAIM. So called by Jacob (Gen. 32:2). Ishbosheth son of Saul was made king there (II Sam. 2:8).

MARI. Capital of the kingdom of Mari on the upper Euphrates. Important for a knowledge of the early Hebrews, though not mentioned in the Bible. Influential in the first part of the 2nd millennium B.C.; destroyed by Hammurabi.

MASADA. Fortress on a hill west of the Dead Sea, scene of the last stand of the Jewish Zealots in the first war with Rome (73 A.D.).

MEGIDDO. Canaanite royal city by the plain of Jezreel, fortified by Solomon (I Kings 9:15). King Josiah was killed there in battle with the forces of Pharaoh Necho (II Kings 23:29).

MEMPHIS. Known to the Jews as Noph from the Egyptian name Men-Nefert. Important city on the Nile and an ancient capital of Lower Egypt. Mentioned several times by the major prophets Isaiah, Jeremiah and Ezekiel.

MICHMASH. Scene of a victory over the Philistines by Jonathan, son of Saul (I Sam. 14).

MODIN. Town of the priest Mattathias, father of Judas Maccabaeus and his brothers, who refused to apostasize from Judaism in the attempt of Antiochus Epiphanes to impose Hellenism on the Jews in 167 B.C. Situated northwest of Jerusalem (I Macc. 2).

NAIN (NAIM). In Galilee south of Nazareth, where Jesus raised a widow's son (Luke 7:11).

NAZARETH (NAZARA). In the New Testament a town of Galilee, home of Joseph and Mary, where Jesus grew to manhood.

NINEVEH. In Mesopotamia on the eastern bank of the Tigris. Ancient city whose foundation is attributed to Nimrod (Gen. 10:11). Royal city of the Assyrian Empire. The prophet Jonah preached against it. Nineveh was overthrown by the Babylonians and their allies in 612 B.C.

NIPPUR. Ancient city of Sumeria. It retained its importance throughout Babylonian history. Records of Jewish interest have been found on the site with other valuable archives. Patron deities En-lil and his consort Nin-lil.

NISIBIS. Influential city of northwestern Mesopotamia noted for its commerce. It played an important part in Assyrian history. In New Testament times Nisibis had a considerable Jewish community, and was a collecting point for gifts sent to the Temple at Jerusalem.

NO-AMON (see **THEBES**).

NOB. A town of the priesthood near Jerusalem where the priest Ahimelech supplied David and his men with hallowed bread when they fled from Saul (I Sam. 21:22). It was a camp of the Assyrian army in their advance on Jerusalem (Isa. 10:32).

NOPH (see **MEMPHIS**).

ON. Ancient Egyptian city northeast of Cairo called Annu. It was a priestly city where was proclaimed the Egyptian pantheon, the companies (**pauti**) of the gods. Joseph married Asenath daughter of Potipherah (Pauti-pe-Ra) priest of On (Gen. 41:45). The city was called by the Greeks Heliopolis (City of the Sun).

PAPHOS. City of Cyprus where St. Paul preached before the governor Sergius Paullus (Acts 13).

PELLA. One of the cities of the Decapolis east of the Jordan. To this region many of the Christians fled during the Jewish war with Rome.

PERGAMUM. City of Mysia in Asia Minor. The Christian community was the recipient of one of the Letters to the Seven Churches (Rev. 2:12). Here was "Satan's seat," the oldest temple of the Roman Emperor worship.

PERSEPOLIS. Royal city of the Persians east of the Persian Gulf, famed for the palace of Darius.

PETRA. In the eastern part of the Arabah, capital city of the Nabataeans. The name, meaning Rock (the city is cut out of sandstone cliffs), makes it probable that it is identical with Sela (rock in Hebrew) city of the Edomites (II Kings 14:7).

PHILADELPHIA (see **RABBATH-AMMON**).

PITHOM. One of the two store-cities of Egypt east of the Delta built by the Israelites, called in Egyptian Pr-Tum, mentioned in Exod. 1:11.

PTOLEMAIS. Coastal city of Palestine, originally the Phoenician Akko (Judg. 1:31). The name was changed by the Graeco-Egyptian king Ptolemy Philadelphus and is mentioned in Acts 21:7. Later known as Acre, reviving the ancient name.

PUTEOLI. Roman port in the bay of Naples to which St. Paul was brought on his way to Rome (Acts 28:13).

QARQAR. Syrian city on the Orontes, where an important battle was fought in 853 B.C. between a Syrian confederacy (which included Ahab king of Israel) and the Assyrians under Shalmaneser.

RABBATH-AMMON. Capital city of the Ammonites where was the great iron bed of Og king of Bashan (Deut.

3:11). Also called Rabbah, besieged by Joab and captured by David (II Sam. 12:26–31). In the Hellenic period the name was changed to Philadelphia, but the ancient association is preserved in the modern name Amman, capital of Jordan.

RAMESES. Store-city of Egypt built by the Israelites (Exod. 1:11), called after the Pharaoh Rameses II.

RAMOTH-GILEAD. City of Gad southeast of the Lake of Galilee. Scene of a battle between the Syrians and Israelites in which Ahab, king of Israel, was killed (I Kings 22). The name gave rise to the Armageddon of Rev. 16:16 (cp. Arimathea for Ramathaim), representing Rama of Gad.

RHODES. City of the Aegean island of this name first ruled by the Dorians and later the Greeks; famed for its colossal statue (about 105 ft. high) of Apollo the sun god, cast in bronze by Chares of Lindus, which stood at the entrance of the harbor from 280-224 B.C. when it was thrown down by an earthquake. Contrary to legend, the legs of the statue were together and did not bestride the harbor entrance. St. Paul's ship called here on his last journey to Jerusalem (Acts 21:1).

RIBLAH. City of Syria on the Orontes, notable for the struggle between Egypt and Babylon in the closing years of the kingdom of Judah (II Kings 23:33, 25:6, 20).

ROME. On the Tiber, founded c.753 B.C., the city which gave its name to the Roman Republic and Empire. Roman history was linked with that of the Jews from the time of the Maccabees, first as ally and later as overlord. The city was built on seven hills (Rev. 17:9) and was regarded by Jews and Christians as the latter-day Babylon. The Great Fire of Rome in 64 A.D. was attributed to the Christians.

SAIS. City of Egypt in the Nile Delta, under the patronage of the goddess Neith. Seat of the Egyptian kings of the 24th and 26th dynasties. Of the latter the Pharaohs Necho and Hophra play a part in Biblical history (II Kings 23; Jer. 44:30).

SALAMIS. In the Bible not the city of Greece but the seaport of Cyprus mentioned in Acts 13:5.

SALEM (see **JERUSALEM**).

SAMARIA. Second capital of the kingdom of Israel built by Omri (I Kings 16:24). The kingdom came to an end with the capture of the city by the Assyrians in 722 B.C. in the reign of Hoshea. In New Testament times the city was embellished by Herod the Great, who changed its name to Sebaste in honor of Augustus (Greek, **Sebastos**).

SARDIS. In Asia Minor, recipient of one of the Letters to the Seven Churches (Rev. 3:1).

SEBASTE (see **SAMARIA**).

SELEUCIA. The port of Antioch on the Orontes from which St. Paul set out on his first missionary journey (Acts 13:4).

SEPPHORIS. Important fortified city of Galilee on a height northwest of Nazareth. It was rebuilt as a Hellenic city by Herod Antipas, and under the Romans became the chief city of Galilee in the period before the Jewish war with Rome.

SHECHEM. Important Canaanite city in the valley between the mountains Ebal and Gerizim visited by Abraham (Gen. 7:6), afterwards a spiritual center of the Israelites. Here Rehoboam son of Solomon lost kingship over Israel (I Kings 12). Shechem became the chief city of the Samaritans. It was destroyed by John Hyrcanus I in 128 B.C., and was rebuilt nearby by the Romans under the name of Flavia Neapolis, from which the modern Nablus is derived. The Hebrew name sometimes appears as Sichem, rendered Sychar in John's Gospel, where Jesus encountered the Samaritan woman (John 4).

SHUSHAN (see **SUSA**).

SIDON. Seaport and Phoenician royal city which had a long and checkered history from early in the 2nd millennium B.C. It was under the patronage of the god Eshmun. Sidon, mentioned several times in the Bible, was closely involved in the struggle between Egypt and Assyria.

SMYRNA. Seaport of Asia Minor (now called Izmir), recipient of one of the Letters to the Seven Churches (Rev. 2:8). It was then an important Roman city north of Ephesus.

SODOM. One of the cities of the plain at the southern end of the Dead Sea. It was destroyed by a catastrophe attributed to the viciousness of its inhabitants. At the time of the overthrow Lot, nephew of Abraham, escaped from the city with his family (Gen. 19).

SUSA. Former capital of Elam and a royal city under the Persians, called Shushan in the Bible. Here lived Nehemiah (Neh. 1:1) and the palace at Susa is the setting of the book of Esther.

SYRACUSE. Ancient seaport and royal city of Sicily, involved in the conflicts of the Greek states and eventually captured by the Romans. Plato lived here for a time, and Syracuse is also famed as the city of the scientist Archimedes and the poet Theocritus. St. Paul landed here on his way to Rome (Acts 28:12).

TARSUS. Chief city of Cilicia on the River Cydnus situated on the south coast of Asia Minor. It was under the patronage of the god Baal-Tarz. Here Mark Antony met Cleopatra of Egypt, and it was the native city of the philosopher Athenodorus, teacher of the Emperor Augustus, and of St. Paul, Saul of Tarsus (Acts 21:39).

TEMPLE OF JERUSALEM. Built by Solomon (I Kings 6), it was later destroyed by the Babylonians in 586 B.C., then rebuilt under the Persians, but less impressively (Hag. 2:3). From 168-165 it was converted by Antiochus Epiphanes into a sanctuary of Zeus Olympios, but restored to Jewish worship by Judas Maccabaeus, who instituted the Feast of Dedication mentioned in John 10:22. Herod the Great reconstructed the Temple in a magnificent manner commencing in 19 B.C. This edifice is described by Josephus (War V.v). It was destroyed by the Romans under the command of Titus in 70 A.D.

THEBES. Royal and priestly city of Upper Egypt on the Nile, under the patronage of the chief god Amun-Re. At various periods it was the capital of Egypt, notably under the 18th, 19th and 20th dynasties (c.1550-1100). Prominent Pharaohs included Amosis I, Queen Hatshepsut, Thutmose III, Amenophis III, Rameses II, Merneptah and Rameses III. The 19th dynasty covered the period of the Exodus and the Israelite invasion of Canaan.

THESSALONICA. City of Macedonia visited by St. Paul (Acts 17). To the church there he addressed the two Epistles to the Thessalonians.

THYATIRA. City of Lydia in Asia Minor. Recipient of one of the Letters to the Seven Churches (Rev. 2:18). Lydia, who welcomed the apostles at Philippi, was from this city (Acts 16:14).

TIBERIAS. City of Galilee on the southwestern shore of the lake built by Herod Antipas and named in honor of the Emperor Tiberius. It was famed for its curative springs. Subsequently it became the chief center of Jewish learning in Palestine, though when first built Jews would not live there as it was partly on the site of a cemetery. There is no record that Jesus entered Tiberias.

TIRZAH. A Canaanite royal city which became the first capital of the separated kingdom of Israel from Jeroboam I to Omri (I Kings 14:16).

TROAS. Otherwise Alexandria-Troas (Trojan Alexandria) on the west coast of Asia Minor, where St. Paul had a vision calling him to Macedonia (Acts 16:9), and later where a young disciple Eutychus fell from a window (Acts 20).

TYRE. A Phoenician royal city built on an island. It played an important part in Phoenician and Syrian history from the 14th century B.C. Hiram I of Tyre was a friend of David and Solomon (II Sam. 5:11; I Kings 5:1). It was famed for the rich dye (Tyrian purple) extracted from the murex shell. Tyre was joined to the mainland by Alexander the Great and it remained prominent throughout the Hellenic period. It is mentioned with Sidon in the Gospels, and St. Paul stayed with the Christians there (Acts 21:3).

UGARIT. Ancient Canaanite city on the coast of Syria which flourished in the 2nd millennium B.C. Literature of the 15th and 14th century discovered here has thrown much light on the Canaanite religion and its reflection in the Bible. Ugarit (modern Ras Shamra) comes into the Tell el-Amarna letters from the time of Pharaoh Akhenaton (middle 14th century). It was destroyed by the "Peoples of the Sea" c.1194 B.C.

UR. Very ancient Sumerian royal city of southern Mesopotamia on the Euphrates near the Persian Gulf. One of its great kings was Ur-Nammu (c.2044–2027 B.C.), author of the oldest known legal code. From this city came the family of Abraham (Gen. 11:27).

ZAREPHATH (SAREPTA). City of Phoenicia associated with a miracle performed by the prophet Elijah (I Kings 17:9; Luke 9:26).

ZOAN (see **AVARIS**).

ZOAR. Formerly Bela, the city to which Lot fled after the destruction of Sodom (Gen. 14:2, 19:22).

ZORAH. In Palestine on the border of the territory of Dan west of Jerusalem, famed as the birthplace of Samson (Judg. 13).

PART IV

DOWN THE CENTURIES

The Bible presents us with the history of a Chosen People, a history which, while it has regard for chronological sequence and for secular events, is related in a way that tends to emphasize spiritual experiences and a Divine purpose. Its information is derived in part from contemporary annals, and there is some reference to circumstances outside the Holy Land where these have a bearing on the narrative. But the Bible is not designed, except incidentally, to satisfy interest in matters unconnected with its objective. Things which the lay historian would regard as momentous happenings may be dismissed in a sentence or not mentioned at all, while others which he would probably omit are dealt with at length. But a certain amount of biblical history has now been amplified and supplemented by archaeological discovery, particularly in Egypt and Mesopotamia, so that drawing on these resources we obtain a more comprehensive picture of what was taking place at different epochs and can observe the movements of peoples and the rise and fall of kingdoms and empires. In this section this is what we shall endeavor in outline to portray.

Throughout the Bible dating is primarily in terms of the lives of men and the reigns of rulers, and is not governed by the employment of eras as a means of reckoning (see Part V, **Calendar and Chronology**). But the definition of various eras from the 8th century B.C. are the great assistance for biblical chronology. Even so, there are few events that can be dated exactly, and most dates have to be treated as approximate, especially prior to 1000 B.C. Disagreement among scholars is still considerable, partly because of insufficient data and conflicting ancient testimonies, so that what can be offered in this respect is a serviceable rough guide.

There are now available written records which take us back to before 3000 B.C., and much of what transpired in the Middle East between 3000 and 2000 B.C. is sufficiently clear to qualify as historical knowledge. But the Bible provides a relatively continuous story only from the time of Abraham. The 2nd millennium B.C. is therefore our best starting point. From this period onward we have increasingly greater insight into developments both in Palestine and the surrounding countries.

2ND MILLENNIUM B.C.

2000-1500. The first half of this millennium saw a considerable movement of semitic peoples. The Amorites controlled much of Mesopotamia, and the first Babylonian Empire was fully established under **HAMMURABI,** 6th Amorite king of the first dynasty of Babylon (c.1724-1682), noted for his **CODE OF LAWS.** From north of Palestine the semitic tide flowed down into Egypt and created the government of the Hyksos from about 1750 to 1570 B.C.

In this period is to be dated the history of the Hebrew **PATRIARCHS.** Migrating from Ur in southern Mesopotamia to Haran in the north, the family of **ABRAHAM** crossed over into Canaan where they led a nomadic life, living in tents. **ABRAHAM** was followed by his son **ISAAC** and his grandson **JACOB.** The rule of the Hyksos in Egypt made it easy for **ABRAHAM** to visit that country, and when **JACOB**'s son **JOSEPH** was sold by his brothers into slavery, and he was taken to Egypt, he was able to rise to the highest position under one of the Pharaohs. It was probably early in the 17th century B.C. that the family of **JACOB** (called **ISRAEL**) settled in Egypt in the eastern frontier region of Goshen.

Egypt reverted fully to native Egyptian rule under **AMOSIS I,** first king of the 18th dynasty, who captured the capital of the Hyksos at Avaris (Tanis) and drove them from the country. About 1510 B.C. **THUTMOSE I,** grandson of **AMOSIS,** carried the war into Palestine, and in the following half century one of the greatest of the Pharaohs **THUTMOSE III** established Egyptian overlordship of Palestine and subjugated much of Syria.

1500-1200. In this period, while the Israelites were in Egypt, an Indo-European people, the Hittites, overcoming the Hurrians in Asia Minor, created an empire covering northern Syria and northern Mesopotamia, which created a serious threat to the Egyptians. Southern Mesopotamia was at this time ruled by the Kassites.

There was a time of relative peace for Egypt at the beginning of the 14th century in the reign of **AMENOPHIS III.** He was a great builder responsible for temples at Karnak and Luxor and the famous Colossi of Memnon. There were widespread diplomatic exchanges throughout the Middle East, largely conducted in a semitic dialect as revealed by the **TELL EL-AMARNA TABLETS** and texts from **UGARIT** in northern Syria. Commerce flourished, and Egyptian and Mycenaean wares were transported by sea and land, finding eager buyers and imitators.

The Egyptian Empire began to crumble, however, under **AMENOPHIS IV** (c.1370-1356) and his son-in-law **TUTANKHAMEN. AMENOPHIS** espoused the cult of Aten in opposition to the dominant worship of Amun-Re, and changed his name to **AKHENATEN.** His simple form of deism was anathema to the powerful hierarchy of Amun, and the king in his reforming zeal little heeded the calls for aid from the rulers of the city-states of Palestine. Semitic **HABIRU** (part of the Hebrew clans related to the Israelites) were pressing southward in association with the Hittites and the forces available could not resist them.

Egyptian hegemony in Palestine was reestablished by the early Pharaohs of the 19th dynasty, **SETI I** and especially his son **RAMESES II** (c. 1301-1234 B.C.). The latter fought a pitched battle with the Hittites and their allies in Syria at Kadesh on the Orontes, and the war ended in 1280 when **RAMESES** and **HATTUSILIS III,** king of the Hittites, entered into a treaty of perpetual friendship.

It appears reasonably certain that **RAMESES II** was the

oppressor of the Israelites, enslaving them and forcing them to build Pithom and Rameses as garrison towns to protect the eastern approaches to Egypt. In his long reign may be placed the birth of **MOSES,** his growth to manhood, and flight to Midian. The Pharaoh of the **EXODUS FROM EGYPT** was probably **RAMESES'** thirteenth son **MERNEPTAH** (1234-1225). This king was closely engaged in the fifth year of his reign with repelling an invasion of Libyan tribes from the west, and this may have given opportunity for the Israelites to escape to the east c. 1230 B.C. A triumphal poem of **MERNEPTAH** has survived recording his victories over the Libyans and the Palestinean peoples, including **ISRAEL.** But his claims, of course, represent his side of the story. It is possible, however, that the Exodus took place about fifteen years earlier while **MERNEPTAH** was acting as effective ruler for his aged father.

The giving of the **TEN COMMANDMENTS** on Mt. Sinai followed the Exodus, and about the end of the period the Israelites after their wanderings in the wilderness were preparing to invade Canaan from the east. **MOSES** died and was succeeded by **JOSHUA.**

1200-1000. At the beginning of this period waves of seaborne migrants from the region of the Aegean bore down upon the coasts of the eastern Mediterranean, among them the Philistines, creating a new peril for Egypt. This invasion of the "Peoples of the Sea" was met and overcome by **RAMESES III** in land and naval battles in 1190, but the Philistines obtained a lodging on the coastal plain north of Egypt which became Philistia. These conditions favored the occupation of parts of Canaan by the Israelites under **JOSHUA.** Crossing the Jordan, victories were won at Jericho and Ai, and especially at the **BATTLE OF HAZOR** where **JOSHUA** defeated a powerful Canaanite confederacy under **JABIN,** king of Hazor.

After **JOSHUA** the tribes of Israel were ruled by **JUDGES,** the most distinguished being **GIDEON, JEPHTHAH, SAMSON** and **SAMUEL.** These were men raised up to deliver the people from subjugation to the peoples of the land, Canaanites, Moabites, Midianites, Amalekites, Amorites, and Philistines in various parts of the country. While they were contending with these opponents the power of Egypt had gravely declined and the empire of the Hittites had come to an end. New powers emerged in the north, the Phoenicians in the coastal region and adjacent to the Aramaeans or Syrians. To the northeast the Assyrians were becoming aggressive, under **TUKULTI-NINURTA I** (1242-1205) and especially under **TIGLATH-PILESER I** (1114-1076).

At this time the spiritual center of Israel was at **SHILOH,** where the **ARK OF THE COVENANT** was kept. The sacred chest was captured by the Philistines at the **BATTLE OF APHEK** (c. 1050). In **SAMUEL'S** old age the people petitioned for a king and **SAUL** of the tribe of Benjamin was chosen (1030-1010). He was killed with his heir **JONATHAN** fighting the Philistines at the **BATTLE OF MT. GILBOA,** and the sovereignty passed to **DAVID** of the tribe of Judah.

1st MILLENNIUM B.C.

1000-900. In the reign of **DAVID** (1010-970), **JERUSALEM** became the civil and spiritual capital of a Hebrew monarchy now in effective control of the country, with neighboring peoples paying tribute. The king of Tyre was an ally. **DAVID** was succeeded by **SOLOMON** (970-931), famed for his wisdom, who built the **TEMPLE** at Jerusalem and brought the kingdom to its maximum prosperity.

Shortly after the accession of **SOLOMON'S** son **REHOBOAM** the kingdom was divided. Ten tribes of Israel followed **JEROBOAM,** who had married a daughter of Pharaoh **SHESHONQ I,** first king of the 22nd dynasty, while Judah and Benjamin remained with **REHOBOAM,** thus creating the separate kingdoms of **ISRAEL** and **JUDAH. REHOBOAM** reigned from 931-913, and **JEROBOAM,** who built a rival sanctuary to Jerusalem at **BETHEL,** from 931-910. In the fifth year of **REHOBOAM** the Temple at Jerusalem was plundered by **SHESHONQ.**

900-800. In this period events in Palestine began to be overshadowed by the growing might of the Assyrian Empire. Cruel and ruthless in their warfare, the Assyrians under **ASHURNASIRPAL II** (884-859), and his son **SHALMANESER III** (859-824), pushed across northern Syria towards the Mediterranean. At first this movement gave little concern further south, where **ASA** of Judah was fighting **BAASHA** of Israel, and getting **BENHADAD I** of Syria to harry Israel from the north. For a few years internal strife affected Israel until **OMRI** (885-874) was established on the throne. **OMRI** changed the capital of Israel from Tirzah to **SAMARIA.**

Near the middle of the century the northern kingdoms, Syria, Israel, Hamath, etc. became temporarily confederate to check the southward progress of the Assyrians. At the **BATTLE OF QARQAR** (853) they confronted the forces of **SHALMANESER.** The result was indecisive, but the Assyrian advance was halted. Assyrian records show that **AHAB,** king of Israel, participated with 2000 chariots and 10,000 soldiers. This king (869-850) was leagued with Phoenicia through his marriage with **JEZEBEL**, daughter of the king of Tyre. In his reign the prophet **ELIJAH** contended against the dominant worship of Baal. **AHAB**, with whom was allied **JEHOSHAPHAT,** king of Judah, was killed fighting the Syrians at the **BATTLE OF RAMOTH-GILEAD.**

A few years later **JEHORAM,** king of Israel, and **JEHOSHAPHAT,** king of Judah, combined to suppress a revolt by **MESHA,** king of Moab. The circumstances from the viewpoint of **MESHA** are recorded on the **MOABITE STELE.** The Assyrians renewed their pressure on the north, and **JEHU,** king of Israel (841-814), became tributary, recorded on the **BLACK OBELISK OF SHALMANESER.** Israel continued tributary under **ADAD-NIRARI III** of Assyria (810-782). The Temple at Jerusalem was repaired in the reign of **JEHOASH,** king of Judah (835-796).

800-700. Between 780 and 740 both Israel and Judah enjoyed a brief increase of power, when **JEROBOAM II** was king of Israel and **AZARIAH** (Uzziah) was king of Judah. The prophetic messages of **AMOS** and **HOSEA** fall in this period, and the ministry of **ISAIAH** began. But the situation quickly deteriorated. Assyrian might was again ascendant under **TIGLATH-PILESER III** (745-727). **REZIN** of Syria and **MENAHEM** of Israel made heavy payments to him to keep their independencies. Both countries tried to get Judah to join them in a defensive alliance, but **AHAZ,** king of Judah, refused for the sake of his own security and called the Assyrians to his aid. **TIGLATH-PILESER** captured Damascus and put an end to the Syrian state in 732. Israel submitted and **HOSHEA** was made puppet king in place of **PEKAH,** but much of its northern territory was annexed.

Israel did not last much longer. **HOSHEA** was unwise enough to revolt against **TIGLATH-PILESER**'s successor **SHALMANESER V,** and tried in vain to obtain help from **SHABAKO** (biblical **SO**) king of Egypt. He was captured, and **SHALMANESER** besieged Samaria, which fell to **SARGON II** in 722. This was the **END OF THE KINGDOM OF ISRAEL.**

At the close of the century **HEZEKIAH** king of Judah (715-687) attempted to appease **SENNACHERIB,** who had ascended the throne of Assyria in 705; but in spite of this the Assyrians invaded Judah and besieged Jerusalem in 701.

700-600. The armies of Assyria suddenly abandoned Judah. There was the hint that the days of this empire were nearly numbered when the king of Babylon, **MERODACH-BALADAN** (Marduk-apal-iddina III), seeking to strengthen himself against Assyria, made overtures to **HEZEKIAH.** Egypt was also staging a comeback, and **TIRHAKAH** (Taharqua), third king of the 25th dynasty from Nubia, was willing to aid Judah. But after the death of **SEN-NACHERIB,** murdered by his sons in 681, the next Assyrian kings, **ESARHADDON** and **ASHURBANIPAL,** sent successful expeditions against Egypt which temporarily relieved any threat from that quarter.

After **HEZEKIAH** the most important Jewish king was **JOSIAH** (637-609), who carried out religious reforms largely inspired by the discovery in the Temple of the **BOOK OF THE LAW.** Contemporary with him an energetic monarch **NABOPOLASSAR** had seized the throne of Babylon. In alliance with the Medes and Scythians he was able to wage effective war against Assyria. The great city of **NINEVEH** was captured and destroyed in 612, and the Assyrians were driven back to the north. This time Egypt under **NECHO II** sought to come to the rescue of the Assyrians. Advancing into Palestine, he was opposed by **JOSIAH,** who fell at the **BATTLE OF MEGIDDO.** The Egyptians swept on to Carchemish on the Euphrates, and the Babylonians barely managed to contain them there. But returning to the struggle under **NEBUCHADNEZZAR,** eldest son of **NABOPOLAS-**

SAR, the Egyptians were decisively defeated at the **BATTLE OF CARCHEMISH** (605).

NEBUCHADREZZAR II (605-562), the Nebuchadnezzar of the Bible, swiftly made himself master of Palestine. **JEHOIAKIM,** placed on the throne of Judah by **NECHO,** became subject to Babylon but later he revolted, refusing to heed the warnings of the prophet **JEREMIAH.**

600-500. NEBUCHADREZZAR crushed the Jewish revolt, captured Jerusalem in 597, and carried off **JEHOIAKIM** and other notables and the vessels of the Temple. Within the year, **JEHOIAKIN** son of **JEHOIAKIM** went into captivity to Babylon, and his brother **ZEDEKIAH** became the last king of Judah. He too revolted in 589, counting on help from **HOPHRA** king of Egypt. This move decided the fate of Judah. Jerusalem was again besieged and captured in 586. The **TEMPLE OF SOLOMON** was destroyed and the **BABYLONIAN EXILE** began. Among the captives was the prophet **EZEKIEL.**

The revived **BABYLONIAN EMPIRE** now achieved its greatest glory under **NEBUCHADREZZAR, NERIGLISSAR** and **NABONIDUS;** but this was short-lived. While **BELSHAZZAR** was regent for his father **NABONIDUS,** the gates of Babylon were opened by treachery to the forces of the Medo-Persians under **CYRUS** in 539.

In the following year an **EDICT OF CYRUS** permitted the exiled Jews to return to their country, and the vessels of the Temple were restored. Led by **ZERUBBABEL,** and encouraged by the prophets **HAGGAI** and **ZECHARIAH,** a Jewish government under Persian suzerainty was established at Jerusalem and work commenced to rebuild the Temple.

The **PERSIAN EMPIRE** was greatly extended. **CAMBYSES** conquered Egypt and his successor **DARIUS I** (522-486) fully organized the empire under provincial governments. Coinage, the Persian Daric, was minted to promote political cohesion and economic development.

500-400. The century opened with Greek resistance to the **PERSIANS,** who were defeated at the **BATTLE OF MARATHON** (490). **XERXES I** (486-465) undertook a massive expedition against the Greeks, who scored another great victory at the **BATTLE OF SALAMIS** (480).

In the reign of **ARTAXERXES I** (465-423), the Jewish official **NEHEMIAH** came from Susa to Jerusalem. It has not been finally determined whether the mission of **EZRA** took place in this reign, or in that of **ARTAXERXES II** (404-358). Greek culture flourished under **PERICLES.** In the second half of the century **SOCRATES** taught. The **PELOPONNESIAN WAR** ended with the fall of Athens (404) when **PLATO** was a young man. After abortive revolts the Egyptians succeeded in throwing off Persian rule in the reign of **DARIUS II** (423-404).

400-300. The reforming government of **EZRA** in Judea and the foundations of the **OLD TESTAMENT CANON** have a place in the first half of this century with the growth of the **SAMARITAN SCHISM.** In Greece we find **PLATO, XENOPHON, DEMOSTHENES** and **ARISTOTLE.** Judea achieved autonomy under a theocratic government of High Priests and Council.

With the rise of Macedonian power under **PHILIP** the foundations were laid for the conquests of **ALEXANDER THE GREAT** (356-323). With a small army **ALEXANDER** crossed the Hellespont in 334 to challenge the might of the Persian Empire under **DARIUS III.** In decisive battles, the **GRANICUS** (334) and **ISSUS** (333), he defeated vastly superior forces, turned south, was welcomed by the Jews, annexed Egypt and laid the foundations of **ALEXANDRIA.** In 331 **ALEXANDER** crossed into Mesopotamia and finally routed the Persians at the **BATTLE OF ARBELA.** He pressed on to the East until he reached the banks of the Indus, bringing together Greek and Indian cultures.

The Macedonian Empire began and ended with **ALEXANDER.** His principal heirs were his generals **PTOLEMY LAGOS** and **SELEUCUS NICATOR.**

300-200. The century was largely taken up with the rivalry between the Ptolemies and the Seleucids. The Ptolemaic dynasty was established in Egypt and at first held Judea. The Seleucid dynasty, established first at Babylon and later at Antioch in Syria, controlled Syria, Babylon and Persia. One of the greatest of the Jewish high priests **SIMEON THE JUST** is believed to have flourished in the first quarter of the century. **PTOLEMY I,** son of **PTOLEMY LAGOS,** founded the museum and library at Alexandria. **PTOLEMY II** (285-247) built the famous lighthouse (**PHAROS**) at Alexandria. In his reign the Greek translation of the Pentateuch (**SEPTUAGINT VERSION**) was undertaken.

Near the middle of the century the Seleucids lost the eastern provinces, but retained a large part of Asia Minor. In the last quarter of the century Palestine was a bone of contention again. The Seleucid king **ANTIOCHUS III** (223-187), assisted by the Jews, seized Palestine and was able to retain it despite defeat by **PTOLEMY IV** (222-205) at the **BATTLE OF RAPHIA** (217). Afterwards peace was concluded between them. Hellenization made considerable progress among the Jews at this period.

In the Mediterranean the **SECOND PUNIC WAR** was raging between the Romans and Carthaginians. **HANNIBAL** crossed the Alps and inflicted heavy defeats on the Romans at the **BATTLE OF LAKE TRASIMENE** (217) and **CANNAE** (216). Rome began a movement to the East in the **MACEDONIAN WARS.**

200-100. The strife between the Seleucids and the Ptolemies continued into this century. Palestine was lost to Egypt by **SELEUCUS IV** (187-175) and regained by **ANTIOCHUS IV** (175-164). Hellenization had so influenced the Jewish hierarchy and nobility that movements of strict loyalty to the Laws of Moses were born, the **CHASIDIM** (Pious) and those afterwards known as **PHARISEES.**

ANTIOCHUS IV (called Epiphanes) determined to compel the Jews to adopt the Greek religion and converted the Temple at Jerusalem to the worship of the Olympian Zeus (168). The sons of the priest **MATTATHIAS** organized a revolt which **JUDAS** called **MACCABAEUS** as their leader. **JUDAS** cleansed the Temple in 165, an event commemorated in the Jewish festival of Dedication (Chanukah). He was killed in battle in 160, and was succeeded in turn by his brothers **JONATHAN** (160-142) and **SIMON** (142-134), who established the **HASMONEAN DYNASTY** holding the high priesthood as well as the civil power. The **PHARISEES** and **SADDUCEES** emerged as opposing religious and political parties, while Chasidism gave rise to the **ESSENES.**

The **THIRD PUNIC WAR** put an end to the power of the Phoenicians in North Africa. **CARTHAGE** fell in 146. The rise of the **ROMAN EMPIRE** began, and before the end of the century had extended to Asia Minor and dominated Egypt.

The Hasmonean dynasty was continued by **JOHN HYRCANUS I** (134-104), whose victories won complete independence for the Jews and enlarged their territory to include

Samaria and the Moabite region beyond Jordan. He was succeeded first by his son **ARISTOBULUS I** (104-103), who added Iturea to his kingdom, and then by another son **ALEXANDER JANNAEUS** (103-76).

100-1. HYRCANUS had rejected the Pharisees in favor of the Sadducees, and this policy was continued by **ALEXANDER.** His reign was troubled by civil war and by the attempt to use to his advantage the strife between **PTOLEMY X** of Egypt and his mother **CLEOPATRA**, who had sought to banish him. **ALEXANDER** when dying advised his wife **SALOME ALEXANDRA** to make peace with the Pharisees to assure the succession. She ruled as regent (76-67) with her elder son **HYRCANUS II** as high priest, but on her death her younger son **ARISTOBULUS II** attempted to seize the throne. There was civil war between them from 67-63. The Romans were brought in and took the side of **HYRCANUS** and Jerusalem surrendered to him and **POMPEY** in 63. Judea became subordinate to Rome.

From 63-40 **HYRCANUS** was nominal ruler, with his friend **ANTIPATER** on behalf of Rome acting as governor of Judea for part of this period. At this time Roman affairs were dominated by the rise and fall of the **FIRST TRIUMVIRATE (CAESAR, CRASSUS** and **POMPEY). JULIUS CAESAR,** conqueror of Gaul and Britain, ultimately defeated **POMPEY** at the **BATTLE OF PHARSALUS** (48). Escaping to Egypt, **POMPEY** was murdered as he landed, and **CAESAR** in turn was assassinated in 44. At the end of the following year the **SECOND TRIUMVIRATE** of **OCTAVIAN, LEPIDUS** and **MARK ANTONY** was formed.

ANTONY, controlling the eastern Roman provinces, came under the influence of **CLEOPATRA** of Egypt in 41. The next year **HEROD,** son of **ANTIPATER,** sponsored by **ANTONY** and **OCTAVIAN** was designated king of Judea by the Roman Senate. But the Parthians invaded Palestine in support of **ANTIGONUS** (40-37), last of the Hasmonean dynasty. With Roman help, **HEROD** returned to Palestine, captured Jerusalem and became king in fact in 37. There followed a struggle for power between **OCTAVIAN** and **ANTONY,** in which the naval forces of **ANTONY** and **CLEOPATRA** were decisively defeated at the **BATTLE OF ACTIUM** (31). To save themselves from dishonorable capture they committed suicide, and Egypt was added to the Roman provinces. **HEROD** had switched his allegiance to

OCTAVIAN and was confirmed in his kingship. **OCTAVIAN** was proclaimed Roman Emperor in 29 and took the title of **AUGUSTUS CAESAR.**

The reign of **HEROD** (37-4) was one of continual fear of plots and conspiracies, which converted him into a bloody tyrant who did not spare to execute his own relations and children. Eager for fame, he erected magnificent edifices, including the rebuilding of the Temple at Jerusalem which was commenced in 19. A year or so before his death **JESUS CHRIST** was born.

The kingdom of **HEROD** was divided between three of his sons, **ANTIPAS, ARCHELAUS** and **PHILIP,** but without the title of king. **ARCHELAUS** obtained Judea and Samaria and **ANTIPAS** Galilee and Peraea.

1ST MILLENNIUM A.D.

1-100. AUGUSTUS deposed **ARCHELAUS,** and Judea and Samaria became part of the Roman province of Syria in 6. The legate of Syria, **QUIRINIUS,** took a census of the Jews for taxation, which roused great opposition, especially by the advocates of Jewish liberty led by **JUDAS OF GALILEE.** The following year **ANNAS** was made high priest. **AUGUSTUS** died in 14 and was succeeded by **TIBERIUS.** A son-in-law of **ANNAS** called **JOSEPH CAIAPHAS** was made high priest in 25. The next year **PONTIUS PILATE** was sent as governor of Judea. Almost immediately he outraged the Jews by letting the Roman forces bring their ensigns into Jerusalem.

About this time **JOHN THE BAPTIST** was preaching repentance in the wilderness of Judea and called upon the Jews to undergo baptism in the Jordan. Among those baptized was **JESUS OF NAZARETH,** who thereafter began to proclaim in Galilee the near advent of the Kingdom of God. **JOHN** was arrested by order of **ANTIPAS** and imprisoned in the fortress of Machaerus beyond Jordan. He had denounced the tetrarch for unlawfully marrying the wife of his half-brother **PHILIP,** but was also regarded as a dangerous agitator. He was executed in prison, but the movement he had founded continued. **JESUS,** who had been teaching and healing in the north and had attracted a considerable following, came to Jerusalem not long after and made a public demonstration as claiming to be the Messiah. The year is uncertain, but perhaps as late as 36. At the time of the Passover he was betrayed by one of his disciples, arraigned as a pretender to the Jewish throne and instigator of revolt against Rome, and condemned by **PONTIUS PILATE** to be crucified.

PILATE, who had behaved harshly towards the Jews and Samaritans, was recalled by **TIBERIUS** in 36. The following year the emperor died and was succeeded by **GAIUS CALIGULA.** There were anti-Jewish riots in Alexandria, and **GAIUS** was readily persuaded to order his statue as Jupiter to be erected in the Temple at Jerusalem. The Jews would have revolted against this outrage, but **PETRONIUS,** legate of Syria, saved the situation by refusing to carry out the emperor's order, and was himself saved from death for disobedience by the assassination of **GAIUS.** By this time the early **CHRISTIAN CHURCH** was well-established in Judea and Samaria in spite of some persecution, and one who had shared in persecuting the followers of Jesus, **SAUL OF TARSUS,** had become a disciple.

On the accession of **CLAUDIUS** as Roman emperor (41-54), he made his friend **AGRIPPA I,** grandson of **HEROD THE GREAT,** king of Judea (41-44). He was the last to hold that office, and on his early death Judea reverted to direct Roman rule, which had the effect of intensifying anti-Roman feeling and activity. In the governorship of **CUSPIUS FADUS** and **TIBERIUS ALEXANDER** the country was placed virtually under martial law. Two sons of **JUDAS OF GALILEE, JAMES** and **SIMON,** were crucified. About this time the Jewish philosopher **PHILO OF ALEXANDRIA** died.

During the decade 46-56 the Messianic movement, both Christian and Jewish, was busy in the eastern part of the Roman Empire and reached Rome itself. **CLAUDIUS** expelled all foreign Jews from Rome because of Messianic agitation and warned Egypt about harboring subversive agents. **SAUL OF TARSUS,** now the Apostle **PAUL,** established many Christian communities in Asia Minor and Greece. **CLAUDIUS** died in 54 and was succeeded by **NERO.**

The folly of the Roman governors of Judea brought the Jews to the brink of revolt. **PAUL,** accused as Christian ringleader, appealed to Caesar and was sent a prisoner to Rome in 60, while **JAMES,** the brother of **JESUS,** was killed in Jerusalem by the pro-Roman party in 62. **PAUL** was probably executed in Rome in 63. The next year the **GREAT FIRE OF ROME** occurred and the Christians were denounced for incendiarism and barbarously executed. Among those who suffered may have been the Apostle **PETER.** In 66 the Jewish inhabitants of Caesarea were massacred, and the revolt against Rome began. Initial success, especially against the forces of the legate of Syria, **CESTIUS GALLUS,** turned the revolt into a full-scale war and a large army was sent by **NERO** under the command of **VESPASIAN.**

In the West, opposition to **NERO** gathered strength. He fled from Rome and committed suicide in 68. In the struggle for power which followed, the imperium was briefly held by **GALBA, OTHO** and **VITELLIUS.** Finally, **VESPASIAN,** acclaimed by the armies of the East, was accepted as emperor in 70. He had returned to Italy from Judea leaving his son **TITUS** to finish the war, by this time in its last stages. Jerusalem was invested by the legions, and at last fell by assault. The Temple was burnt down in August of 70, and the defenders weakened by famine were massacred. But Jewish resistance was not completely overcome until the fortress of Masada near the Dead Sea fell in 73.

Many of the Jewish followers of **JESUS** had succeeded earlier in escaping from Jerusalem across the Jordan. These reorganized the Nazorean section of the Church under the leadership of **SIMEON, SON OF CLEOPHAS,** a cousin of **JESUS,** who is said to have lived until the reign of **TRAJAN.**

VESPASIAN died in 79, and **TITUS** reigned only two years. At his death in 81 he was succeeded by his brother **DOMITIAN.** Christianity was treated as an illegal and subversive religion, but continued to make converts in spite of increased persecution. **DOMITIAN** was assassinated in 96, and his successor **NERVA** died in 98 when **TRAJAN** became emperor. By the time of his reign all the **FOUR GOSPELS** were in existence.

PART V

SOCIAL AND ECONOMIC LIFE

Calendar and Chronology—Coins and Money—Costume—Musical Instruments—Ranks and Titles—Weights and Measures.

The reader of the Bible inevitably comes across many things which are of incidental interest rather than of special consequence. These may relate to almost any circumstance connected with the life of the people in Bible lands at different epochs. An article is mentioned, a weight, or a coin; or it may be the name of a month or the title of an official, which being unfamiliar arouses curiosity. The terms encountered, when their meaning and associations are understood, help to illustrate conditions and usages, and thus to visualize the personalities of the Bible in their native environment. Often biblical films and pictures are misleading because they are filled with inaccuracies. The subjects represented here and in Part VI have been selected as being among the most useful as a guide to biblical references. Together they range over a variety of aspects of spiritual, social and economic life in the ancient world.

AGES (ARCHAEOLOGICAL). Different materials for tools and weapons came into use in successive periods in various parts of the world, providing archaeologists with a convenient rough system for dating cultures. The system given here relates to excavations in Palestine. The figures to the nearest hundred years must be treated as approximations, and styles of pottery permit of further and more exact subdivisions important for the specialist.

Neolithic (New Stone) Age	6000–4500 B.C.
Chalcolithic (Copper-Stone) Age	
Early	4500–4000
Middle	4000–3500
Late	3500–3200
Bronze Age	
Early	3200–2100
Middle	2100–1500
Late	1500–1200
Iron Age	
Early	1200–1000
Middle	1000–900
Late	900–600

AGES (BIBLICAL). The Bible uses the term Age (**olam, eon**) to signify great units of time of unspecified length, translated sometimes as "ever" or "everlasting." Major time cycles were known to the ancient astronomers of the Middle East, but it is not clear that the biblical "Ages" should be identified with any of them. (See also **ASTRONOMICAL OBSERVATION** and **WORLD-WEEK**).

ASTRONOMICAL OBSERVATION. The night sky of the Middle East could not fail to inspire astronomical study and spiritual inquiry. "When I consider thy heavens, the work of thy fingers, the moon and the stars, which thou hast ordained; what is man, that thou art mindful of him?" (Ps. 8:3). Over thousands of years observation was maintained and records were kept, so that considerable knowledge was acquired of the cosmic cycles and the movements of the heavenly bodies, the uncountable hosts of heaven. The sun and the moon were the great lights respectively of day and night, while the seven planets ruled the stars. Eclipses could accurately be predicted, and the phenomena of comets, shooting stars and meteorite showers, were noted and given spiritual interpretation. Astrology went hand in hand with astronomy. The casting of horoscopes was a venerable art, and events on earth were held to be mapped out in the heavens for the skilled to discern. The zodiacal almanac was an old invention. Monotheistic Judaism accepted the existence of the spiritual forces of the skies, but repudiated their polytheistic significance.

CREATION, ERA OF. The mode of reckoning years from the Creation (A.M.—**Anno Mundi**) was not introduced among the Jews until the 3rd century A.D. and did not become customary before the Middle Ages. By this reckoning the year of Creation equated with 3760 B.C. An earlier attempt in the 2nd century B.C. was made by the Zadokite Essenes to change the Hebrew calendar from a lunar to a solar year and to base chronology on a system of jubilees (7 years and 49 years) as shown in the **Book of Jubilees.** This system also dated from the Creation, but was employed only by sectarians. (For other systems of chronology see **DATING EVENTS** and **ERAS**).

DATING EVENTS. Before the introduction of dating by eras reckoning was associated with natural phenomena like eclipses and earthquakes (Amos 1:1), the years of the reign of kings, which was more systematic, or other outstanding circumstances (Num. 13:22; Isa. 10:1). Of great assistance in the determination of Old Testament chronology was the discovery of the Assyrian Eponymous List and the Babylonian Chronicle.

DAY AND NIGHT, DIVISIONS OF. Among the Hebrews day followed night (Gen. 1:4), and holy days were from evening to evening. Day was from sunrise to sunset, and night from sunset to sunrise. The subdivision of day and night into 12 periods each (hours) came from the Babylonians, who also introduced minutes. But hours only appear in the New Testament. The Jews divided the night into three watches, evening, midnight and morning (Exod. 14:24; Judg. 7:19; I Sam. 11:11; Luke 12:28). The Romans had four watches, evening, midnight, cockcrow, and morning (Mark 6:48, 13:35).

ERAS. The reckoning of time by eras did not affect Jewish chronology until after the return from the Babylonian Exile. Some Jews would be acquainted with the Babylonian Era (Era of Nabonasser) dating from 747 B.C. and later with the Greek reckoning by the Olympic Games held every four years, making one Olympiad, commencing from 776 B.C. Still later they must have known the Roman Era (A.U.C., year of the foundation of the city of Rome) corresponding to 753 B.C., though some Roman historians make it a year or two earlier. But the civil era actually used in Palestine from the second century B.C. was the Seleucid or Macedonian Era. This was called by the Jews the Era of Kings and Era of Contracts, since they were required by the Syrian governors to employ it in dating civil contracts. This era began in 312 (311) B.C., the year of the occupation of Babylon by Seleucus Nicator. The Christian Era, introduced in the 6th century A.D., commenced on January 1, after the assumed date of the birth of Christ, corresponding to the 4th year of the 194th Olympiad and the 753rd of the foundation of Rome. This era is several years out, since Jesus was born before the death of Herod the Great in 4 B.C. according to the Gospel of Matthew.

GEZER CALENDAR. For the peasant farmer of Palestine the year in ancient times was represented not so much by the official months as by the seasonal tasks to be performed. He would speak of an event as happening at the time of the wheat harvest (Gen. 30:14), or the barley harvest (II Sam. 11:9), or the summer fruit harvest (Isa. 16:9). This is illustrated by a limestone tablet found at Gezer dating from about 900 B.C., inscribed in Hebrew with a list of the tasks for the different seasons of the year, including sowing and pruning and the harvesting of the various crops.

INTERCALATION. In ancient Egypt the year consisted of 12 months, each of 30 days, making 360 days. To bring this into line with the solar year of 365 days, five year-end days were added associated with the birthdays of the divinities Osiris, Horus, Set, Isis and Nephythys. The Babylonians, on the other hand, in earlier times had a similar year of 360 days, adding an intercalcated 13th month when necessary, to link with the solar year. Later they adopted a lunar year of 354 days consisting of 12 months in which a month of 29 days alternated with one of 30 days, again intercalcating an extra month periodically to equalize with the solar year. This system was followed by the Jews in the time of the Second Temple. It is not certain what their system was in earlier times.

JUBILEES. The Mosaic Code provided not only for a weekly seventh day Sabbath, but also for a Sabbath for the land every seventh year. After seven times seven years there followed a fiftieth Jubilee year. These intervals were concerned also with the release of Hebrews who might have sold themselves into bondage and the restoration of land to its former family ownership (Lev. 25).

LUNAR-SOLAR YEAR (see **INTERCALCATION**).

MONTHS. Both in Egypt and Mesopotamia the year was divided into 12 months, and this system was employed by the Hebrews. Only four of the early month names are given in the Bible, the first month Abib, the second Ziw, the seventh Ethanim, and the eighth Bul. After the Babylonian Exile the names in use followed those of Mesopotamia; but under the Seleucid kings the Macedonian names were largely used for civil purposes. Both are listed below. (See also **NEW YEAR** and **SEASONS**).

Jewish	*Macedonian*	*English*
Nisan	Xanthicus	April
Iyyar	Artemisius	May
Sivan	Daesius	June
Tammuz	Panemus	July
Ab	Loüs	August
Ellul	Gorpiaeus	September
Tishri	Hyperberetaeus	October
Cheshvan	Dius	November
Kislev	Apellaeus	December
Tevet	Audynaeus	January
Shevat	Peritius	February
Adar	Dystrus	March

In a leap year the Jewish calendar adds an extra month, Ve-Adar or Adar Sheni (Second Adar).

NEW MOON. Prior to the Babylonian Exile the New Moon was observed as a public holiday equal in importance to the Sabbath (I Sam. 20:18; II Kings 4:23; Amos 8:5). The day was heralded by the blowing of trumpets and special sacrifices were offered. While some of the practices continued in the time of the Second Temple the observation of the New Moon was chiefly of consequence for purposes of the sacred calendar in determining the commencement of the major festivals.

NEW YEAR. Two modes of reckoning the New Year are present in the Bible. Anciently the year commenced in the autumn, which was the beginning of the agricultural year, and the first of Tishri is still Jewish New Year's Day in the sacred calendar. Later, in keeping with Babylonian custom, Nisan in the spring was made the first month of the secular year, associated with the Passover commemoration of the exodus from Egypt.

SACRED YEAR. Other holy days are described or mentioned in the Bible as well as New Moons and Sabbaths. The principal are the following:

Nisan 14	Eve of the Passover.
Nisan 15	Feast of Unleavened Bread (seven days).
Sivan 6	Pentecost (Feast of Weeks).
Tishri 1	New Year (Feast of Trumpets).
Tishri 10	Day of Atonement (Fast Day).
Tishri 15	Feast of Tabernacles (Ingathering), for eight days.
Tishri 21	Hoshana Rabba (Great Hosanna).
Tishri 22	Eighth Day of Solemn Assembly

ADDITIONS IN NEW TESTAMENT TIMES

Kislev 25	Feast of Dedication (Feast of Lights), celebrating the restoration of Temple worship by the Maccabees (eight days).
Adar 13	Purim (Feast of Lots, or of Esther), commemorating the deliverance of the Jews recorded in the book of Esther.

Passover, Pentecost, and Tabernacles were pilgrim festivals, because on these occasions the people made a pilgrimage to the Temple at Jerusalem. The minor holy days and intermediate days of festivals did not involve cessation of labor unless they fell on a Sabbath. In New Testament times a number of days of national consequence, such as Nicanor's Day, were listed as dates in which fasting was forbidden.

SEASONS. The Egyptians divided their year of twelve months into three seasons of four months each, commencing in mid-July. The Hebrew agricultural year began in October and consisted also of three seasons, Winter, Spring, and Summer.

WEEK. The Hebrew week did not name the days, but numbered them, the first day corresponding to Sunday. The seventh day was also called the Sabbath, a word taken from the Babylonians, with whom however it was not the seventh day. In late usage Friday was known as the Preparation Day (for the Sabbath) or Eve of the Sabbath. The Babylonian week was named after the planets in the order Sun, Moon, Mars, Mercury, Jupiter, Venus, Saturn.

WORLD-WEEK. This was an eschatological and cosmic conception derived from the Iranian idea of the conflict between the Good and Evil Powers which would last for twelve millennia. Some Jewish sects of the time of Christ thought of the world as lasting for a week of millennia, the seventh (Sabbatical) being represented by the Messianic Era of a thousand years ("one day is with the Lord as a thousand years"). Another way of dividing the World-Week was into periods: 2000 years without Law, 2000 years under Law, and 2000 years of preparation for the Kingdom of God, which would govern the world in the 7th millennium.

COINS AND MONEY

Before the Babylonian Exile money was reckoned by weight. Coinage was not introduced until the Persian period, and not to any appreciable extent in Palestine until after the time of Alexander the Great in the 3rd century B.C. The first Jewish ruler given the right to mint coinage was Simon Maccabaeus (142-134 B.C.) according to I Macc. 15:6. In earlier times monetary transactions were in gold and silver bars or rings, the recognized weights being those of the Babylonian system, namely 60 shekels = 1 mina, 60 minas = 1 talent. Later a weight of 50 shekels to the mina was adopted. The Phoenician shekel of silver was slightly lighter in weight than the Babylonian and was commonly used in Palestine. Since transactions in silver were most usual for ordinary daily purposes the Hebrew word for it, **kesef,** had the meaning of money. The shekel of silver was subdivided into half and quarter shekels, and even twentieths of a shekel known as a gerah or obol (Gen. 24:22; I Sam. 9:8; Exod. 30:13).

The establishment of coinage brought a great variety into currency, cities and provinces minting their own, and the lucrative business of money changer became essential for commerce. For small money, copper and bronze came into use. The coinage system provided an excellent medium of publicity in the ancient world, rather similar to that of the postage stamp today, creating a public image of emperors, kings and governors, calling attention to their laws, policies and victories, lauding the dignity of cities and publicizing their chief attractions. Jewish coinage was notably simple, and in obedience to Jewish law bore no representation of man or beast. For offerings in the Temple no coin could be accepted which violated this law or made any reference to heathen divinities. The half-shekel Temple tax weighed 112.2 grains.

ASSAR (Gr. **assarion**), a bronze coin, translated farthing (Matt. 10:29), about one twenty-fourth of a denarius.

AUREUS, a gold coin struck under the Roman Empire worth 25 denarii, not mentioned in the New Testament.

DARIC (gold stater), struck by Darius I, Persian coin about the same value as the Roman aureus, translated dram (I Chron. 29:7).

DENARIUS (Gr. **denarion**), the standard Roman silver coin equal to about 10 cents, translated penny (Matt. 22:18), the average day's pay for a farm laborer in Palestine (Matt. 20:20).

DRACHMA, a Greek silver coin (Luke 15:8) approximately equal to the denarius. The didrachm (double drachma) as equal to the helf-shekel of the Temple tax, the tribute money of Matt. 17:24, while the tetradrachm (quadruple drachma or stater) equalled one shekel, the tax for two persons (Matt 17:27).

GERAH (Gr. **obol**), weight, value of one twentieth of a shekel (Ezek. 45:12).

LEPTON, smallest Greek bronze coin, equal to one ninety-sixth of a denarius, translated mite (Mark 12:42).

MINA, not a coin but money value equal to 100 denarii, translated pound (Luke 19:13).

PERUTAH, Hebrew equivalent of the lepton (ref. the **Mishnah**).

QUADRANS (Gr. **kodrantes**), equal to one sixty-fourth of a denarius, translated farthing (Matt. 5:26).

SESTERTIUS, Roman coin equal to one quarter of a denarius, not mentioned in the New Testament.

SHEKEL, Jewish silver coin equal to the tetradrachm. Half-shekels in silver were also struck, and in the revolt of Bar Cochba brass quarter-shekels.

STATER (otherwise tetradrachm; see **DRACHMA**).

TALENT, not a coin but money value equal to 6000 denarii (Matt. 18:24). (See also section on **Weights and Measures**).

COSTUME

Our knowledge of costume of the Hebrews is far from adequate, depending on a few representations on Egyptian and Assyrian monuments and some biblical references. From monumental sources and paintings we are much more familiar with the peoples with whom the Israelites and later the Jews were in contact: Egyptians, Babylonians, Assyrians, Hittites, Philistines, Syrians, Persians, Greeks and Romans. From period to period the styles of various articles of apparel would be imitated by the Hebrews from their neighbors; but they also had typical clothing.

PATRIARCHAL AGE. The common costume was the tunic fastened over one shoulder. With men this was knee-length, while the women wore theirs down to the ankles. Some men had only a short skirt with bare torso. Sandals were worn by some, though many went barefoot, and women had head scarves with which they could veil themselves. Dress material was principally woven wool with bright patterns of many colors (Gen. 37:3). Linen was favored by the well-to-do.

MONARCHY. In the northern kingdom of Israel the common costume was a full-length tunic with girdle, over which the men wore a fringed mantle. Their heads were covered with gnome-like caps of wool, kept in place by a fillet: the fillet was often worn as a headband without the cap. Shoes were in use and also the high boot like that of the Hittites. In the southern kingdom of Judah, costume was similar, namely tunic and mantle. The wardrobe of fashionable women is listed in Isa. 3:18–25.

TIME OF CHRIST. The Jews of Palestine wore tunics and cloaks like the Greeks, but distinguished by the obligatory fringe in which was inserted a blue thread or tassel, and some wore the ankle-length robe. It is probable that the Greek hat and Phrygian cap were in use. The Jews were not dressed like Arabs as commonly depicted in illustrations of Gospel scenes.

MUSICAL INSTRUMENTS

From very early times singing was accompanied by musical instruments of a rudimentary character in the three divisions of strings, wind and percussion. By the 2nd millennium B.C. a considerable variety existed, especially of stringed instruments, as we may see from the wall paintings of Egypt and the sculptures of Mesopotamia. In Palestine some of these were perhaps cruder, but most kinds are mentioned in the Bible with a notable, though late, short list in Daniel 3:5. Musical directions are provided in the headings of several of the Psalms, though the implications are not always clear, and instrumental accompaniment was a feature of the singing of the great Temple choirs. Music entered intimately into the life of the people in times of joy and sorrow. The identification of instruments in the King James Version is not always correct, and can now to a considerable extent be improved upon in the light of further knowledge. Allowance has of course to be made for differences in the instruments of the various countries concerned and at widely separated periods. Some of the Hebrew words are onomatopoeic.

BELL (Heb. **metsillah**). Bells were attached to clothing to give a pleasant tinkling sound in movement, and were also attached to the harness of horses (Zech. 14:20).

BRASS (in the expression "sounding brass" I Cor. 13:1), a bronze gong.

CORNET. Three different words are so translated: (1) **keren,** also translated horn; (2) **shofar,** also translated trumpet; and (3) **maneaneim** (see under **SISTRUM**). The first two relate to short and long trumpets of horn.

CYMBALS. Two round metal plates clashed together (Heb. **metsiltayim**) as in I Chron. 13:8, and a cuplike type (**tseltsilim,** II Sam. 6:5) with one part brought down on the other held steady in the hand.

DRUM (Heb. **toph**). A small hand drum tapped with the fingers, translated timbrel and tabret (see **TABRET**).

DULCIMER (Aram. **sumphonyah**). The Babylonians had a stringed instrument which fitted to the waist of the player leaving both hands free, and this had a skin stretched below to form a sounding board. Some authorities render the Hebrew word as bagpipes (Dan. 3:5).

FLUTE (Aram. **mashroqitha**). Possibly a kind of pan-pipes (Dan. 3:5). This wind instrument is perhaps the same as the **ORGAN** (Heb. **ugab**, Gen. 4:21).

GUITAR (or **LUTE**). An instrument of this type is shown in Egyptian illustrations.

HARP (Heb. **kinnor**). A great variety of harps were used in ancient times from small hand harps to full size, often elaborately ornamented, instruments. The number of strings also varied up to a maximum of ten strings (Ps. 92:3). With some harps the plectrum was used. Another word translated harp (Dan. 3:5; I Cor. 14:7) is the **kithara** (see **LYRE**).

LYRE (Heb. **nebel**). This word is variously translated **PSALTERY** and **VIOL** in the Old Testament. It may well have been like the Egyptian lyre, held horizontally and having a sounding board of wood. This type commonly had seven strings. The Greek U-shaped lyre (**kithara**) was held upright and had three or five strings.

ORGAN (see **FLUTE**).

PAN-PIPES (see **FLUTE**).

PIPES (Heb. **chalil**). Single and double pipes of reed were in use (I Sam. 10:5; I Cor. 14:7). There were also bagpipes consisting of two pipes joined to a goatskin bag (see **DULCIMER**).

PSALTERY. A kind of hand harp or lyre (see **LYRE**). In Dan. 3:5 the reference (Aram. **psanterin**) is to a kind of **DULCIMER.**

SACKBUT (Aram. **sabbeka**). A three-sided instrument with four strings (Dan. 3:5).

SISTRUM. A kind of rattle giving a tinkling sound. The common Egyptian type consisted of a flat loop, through which loose horizontal rods were inserted, attached to a handle. Translated **CORNET** in II Sam. 6:5.

TABRET (TIMBREL). Types of tambourine (Heb. **toph**) commonly used with pipes to accompany dancing. Egyptian illustrations depict round and oblong varieties.

TRUMPET (Heb. **hatzotzerah**). For the sacred services silver trumpets were used. These were long straight instruments with bell mouths. At a later time bronze trumpets were common. For horn trumpets see **CORNET.**

VIOL (Heb. **nebel**). A kind of hand harp (see **LYRE**).

RANKS AND TITLES

The Bible makes reference to a number of officials, military commanders, and persons of rank and quality. It also gives certain titles of honor conferred on rulers and persons of distinction. The names in the various categories are not only from Hebrew and Greek usages, but also in some cases from Assyrian, Egyptian, Persian and Roman. Sometimes the significance is quite clear, e.g., king and high priest, but in others the rendering of the King James Version does not convey the real meaning, and occasionally an office or title is left untranslated. The lists which follow are divided into Old Testament and New Testament sections and cover all but the more obvious of the Biblical references. The lists do not include trades and professions, but a few offices are mentioned which would be familiar to Jews though not in the Bible.

Old Testament

BEEL-TEEM, translated **CHANCELLOR** (Ezra 4:8), probably Chief of Intelligence.

CAPTAIN, leader or military officer as listed.

CHAMBERLAIN (see **SARIS**).

CHANCELLOR (see **BEEL-TEEM**).

COUNSELLOR. Several different terms give the sense of Adviser or Counsellor, including references to court officials. The words Wonderful Counsellor (Isa. 9:6) should be taken as an honorific title.

DUKE (Gen. 36:15), chieftain, head of a thousand or family.

EVERLASTING FATHER (Isa. 9:6). Literally, Father of Eternity. Eastern rulers were honorifically described as living forever (Dan. 2:4).

FATHER TO PHARAOH (Gen. 45:8). Expression representing the Egyptian "Father of the Divine One" (i.e., Pharaoh), honorific title of a high priestly officer of state.

JUDGE (Heb. **Dayyan**), distinguished from Magistrate (**Shophet**).

KAR, translated **CAPTAIN** (II Kings 11:4), an uncertain term possibly relating to the royal bodyguard.

MAGISTRATE (Heb. **Shophet**).

MIGHTY GOD (Isa. 9:6), better rendered as the honorific Mighty Hero.

NAGID, leader or ruler (I Sam. 25:30).

NASI, prince (most commonly).

NATSAB, translated officer or deputy, better rendered as Commissioner.

PAQID, inspector or overseer.

PECHAR, governor or viceroy (I Kings 10:15).

PHARAOH, title of Egyptian sovereigns, meaning the Great House.

QATSIN, ruler or captain, better rendered Authority.

RAB (CAPTAIN).

RAB-MAG (Jer. 39:13). Title of a Babylonian official.

RAB-SARIS (Jer. 39:13). Title of a Babylonian official, possibly **rabu-sa-resu** meaning Comptroller.

RAB-SHAKEH (II Kings 18:17). Title of an Assyrian official, **rab-shaqu,** a high King's Agent, also of the governor of the province east of Harran.

ROSH (CHIEF).

SAR, usually translated prince or **CAPTAIN,** better rendered Commander and applying to all grades of officers, Commander-in-chief, Commander of an Army, down to Commanders of 1000 men, 100, 50 or less. The significance of king or prince was in keeping with the military implication of the term.

SARIS, CHAMBERLAIN and eunuch, domestic palace official (Esth. 1:10).

SATRAP, translated lieutenant, but actually various grades of governor in the Persian Empire.

SEGAN (Ezra 9:2), local governor or prefect.

SEREN (Josh. 13:3), a lord, always in connection with the Philistines.

SHERIFF (Tiphtaye), a Babylonian official associated with local communities.

SHOPHET (see **MAGISTRATE).**

SHOTER, usually translated officer, an overseer or supervisor.

SON OF GOD, honorific title of kings as earthly representatives of deity. Among polytheistic peoples it credited divinity to kings.

TARTAN (Assyr. **Turtanu**), title of Generalissimo of the Assyrian forces (II Kings 18:17).

TIRSHATHA, Persian official, title of the Governor of Judea (Ezra 2:63).

New Testament

ARCHISYNAGOGOS, president of a local Jewish community, translated ruler of the synagogue (Mark 5:22).

ARCHON, ruler, used also of cosmic spiritual powers.

AREOPAGITES (Areopagite), member of the Athenian court of religion and morals meeting on Mars Hill, the Areopagus (Acts 17:34).

ASIARCH (Chief of Asia, Acts 19:31), elected presidents and patrons of the festivals and games at Ephesus, also associated with the Imperial cult.

AUGUSTUS (Gr. **Sebastos**), meaning revered one, honorific name assumed by Octavian on becoming emperor of the Romans and adopted by subsequent emperors of this line (Luke 2:1; Acts 25:21).

BOULEUTES (see under **COUNSELLOR**).

CAESAR, designation of the Roman Emperor after Julius Caesar.

CENTURION, Roman commander of 100 men.

CHAMBERLAIN, Chief Eunuch (Acts 12:10), City Treasurer (Rom. 16:23).

CHILIARCH, commander of 1000 men, usually translated Chief Captain, Greek equivalent of Roman Military Tribune (Acts 21:13).

CONSUL. Roman Chief Magistrate exercising the Imperial prerogatives. Not mentioned in the Bible.

COUNSELLOR (Mark 15:43).

DEACON (Gr. **Diakonos**), an administrator, usually translated minister.

EPISKOPOS, a supervisor (bishop).

EPITROPOS, translated Steward (Luke 8:3), better rendered Chancellor.

ETHNARCH, ruler of a nation, office held by Archelaus successor to Herod the Great, and less sovereign than king.

GOVERNOR (Gr. **Hegemon**). The Roman Governor of the Province of Syria was a Legatus (Legate), while the subordinate Governor of Judea was only a Procurator (Matt. 27:2). The Roman Governor of Egypt was a Praefectus (Prefect).

MAGISTRATE (see **PRAETOR**).

MARI (Aram. Lord). In I Cor. 15:22, **Maran** (our **Lord**).

MESSIAH (Gr. **Christos**), the Anointed One, applied to Jewish high priests and kings who underwent ritual anointing on taking office. Thus particularly applied to the expected final Deliverer of Israel of the royal line of David and Vicegerent of God, Jesus the Christ.

OFFICER (Gr. **Hyperites**), a minor officer or servant. In Luke 12:58 a police officer or bailiff (Gr. **Praktor**).

POLITARCHS, translated rulers of the city, city prefects (Acts 17:6).

PONTIFEX MAXIMUS. Priestly office held by the Roman Emperors. The office was concerned with fixing the religious calendar, appointment of Vestal Virgins and Flamens, etc. The title appeared on the imperial coinage, but is not mentioned in the Bible.

PRAETOR, magistrate (Acts 16:20), a Roman official.

PROCONSUL, Roman office described as Deputy (Acts 18:12).

PUBLICAN, a Roman official acting as tax collector (Matt. 5:46).

RABBI, in the time of Christ a Jewish honorific title of esteem for learning. Also **Rabban** (our Rabbi).

SEGAN, not used in the New Testament, but current in the time of Christ as the title of the deputy for a high Jewish official, like English Vice-President.

STRATEGOS, translated magistrate (see **PRAETOR**).

TETRARCH, ruler of a region consisting of four territories, but the Greek word taken over by the Romans was often given to rulers having a lower status than that of king. They were sometimes addressed as king by courtesy.

TRIBUNE, MILITARY (see **CHILIARCH**).

TOWN CLERK (Acts 19:35), the City Recorder.

THEOLOGOS, in Greek usage Spokesman of a God, taken over to express the function of the seer of the Revelation (St. John the Divine).

WEIGHTS AND MEASURES

WEIGHTS. In the section on **Coins and Money** it has been pointed out that before the late introduction of coinage, monetary transactions were on a basis of weight, commonly of silver. The Hebrew weights closely followed the Babylonian, consisting of the shekel, the mina, and the talent. Earlier 60 shekels made up a mina, and 60 minas a talent; later the proportion of 50 shekels to a mina was adopted. The shekel was subdivided into the half-shekel (**beka**), quarter-shekel, and twentieth-shekel (**gerah or obol**).

It is important, however, that under the Babylonian system there were two standards, the "regal" and the "popular," the regal being somewhat heavier, and each was subdivided into a "heavy" form, and a "light" form which was half the weight of the heavy. The standard prevailing in Palestine and Syria was the popular standard in its heavy form. The approximate respective weights are shown in the following table.

Regal Heavy	*Regal Light*
1 shekel = 16.37 grams	1 shekel = 8.41 grams
1 mina = 1010 grams	1 mina = 505 grams
1 talent = 60,600 grams	1 talent = 30,300 grams
Popular Heavy	*Popular Light*
1 shekel = 16.37 grams	1 shekel = 8.16 grams
1 mina = 982.4 grams	1 mina = 491.2 grams
1 talent = 58,944 grams	1 talent = 29,472 grams

The change from 60 to 50 shekels to the mina made the weight of the mina 818.6 grams, equal to 2½ Roman pounds, and the weight of the talent (3000 shekels) 49,110 grams. The Phoenician shekel used for silver weighed 14.55 grams, and this was employed when coinage was introduced, making the mina of 50 monetary shekels equal to 727.5

grams, and the talent of 3000 monetary shekels equal to 43,659 grams. But this did not affect weights other than in currency.

MEASURES (Length). The primitive system of measurement was derived from the human limbs, such as the fingerbreadth; the handbreadth, represented by the breadth of the four fingers; the span of roughly the length from elbow to wrist; and the ell, or cubit, from elbow to the finger tips. The feet provided the measurement of a "step" (I Sam. 20:3) or "pace" (II Sam. 6:13). Apart from the human body, a reed was found to be roughly the length of six forearms, and longer distances were suggested by a "bowshot" (Gen. 21:16) and a "stone's throw" (Luke 22:41). The biblical system gives the following table:

4 fingerbreadths = 1 handbreadth
3 handbreadths = 1 span
2 spans = 1 cubit
6 cubits = 1 reed

When measurement became more precise, the standard was provided by fixing the length of the cubit. As with weights, however, there was a greater Regal and a lesser Popular. The Regal cubit of Israel was 7 handbreadths (Ezek. 40:5) as against the Popular 6 handbreadths. The cubit was also reckoned differently in Babylonia and Egypt, thus:

BABYLONIA

Regal	1 cubit = 55 cm. (21.6 in.)
Popular	1 cubit = 49.5 cm. (19.5 in.)

EGYPT

Regal	1 cubit = 52.5 cm. (20.7 in.)
Popular	1 cubit = 45 cm. (17.7 in.)

It is regarded as most probable that the length of the Hebrew cubit was similar to that of the Egyptians, about 17⅔ inches for the Popular, and one sixth longer for the Regal, especially as in New Testament times it was accommodated to the Greek cubit of 17½ inches. The distance of a Sabbath day's journey was 2000 cubits.

The additional measurements of length found in the New Testament are the Greek furlong (**stadion**) = 600 Greek feet

(194 yards), though there was also a longer furlong; and the mile (Matt. 5:41) = 5000 Roman feet (about 1617 yards).

MEASURES (Area). The measurements of area for land given in the Bible are not precise. Two methods of calculation are mentioned, the "yoke acre" (Isa. 5:10) representing the area which could be ploughed in a day by a yoke of oxen, and the "seed area" (Lev. 27:16) of various dimensions reckoned according to the amount of barley seed required to sow it. The Egyptian acre was the square of 100 Regal cubits, equal to between half and two-thirds of an acre. The Hebrew acre was probably the same. The squaring system was used by the Hebrews (Exod. 28:16), the length of two sides being given.

MEASURES (Capacity). The tables which follow give the Hebrew measures referred to in the Bible with approximate modern equivalents, the capacities being those which prevailed in New Testament times. As the cubit provided the standard for measurements of length so did the ephah or bath for those of capactiy. It is likely that ephah represented a lesser quantity in the Old Testament period.

Dry Measure

1 log = 4 cabs (1 cab = 3.66 pints)
6 cabs = 1 seah (2.74 gallons)
3 seahs = 1 ephah (8.22 gallons)
10 ephahs = 1 homer or cor (82.19 gallons)

The ephah was also divided into 10 parts, omer or issaron (Num. 28:5).

Liquid Measure

1 log = 1.06 pints
12 logs = 1 hin (12.67 pints)
6 hins = 1 bath (as 1 ephah)

The New Testament gives the Greek for certain Hebrew terms and adds one or two others in current use in the Greco-Roman world.

BATOS (bath) translated "measure" (Luke 16:6) = 9.58 gallons.

CHOENIX translated "measure" (Rev. 5:6) = 2.2 pints.

KOROS (cor) translated "measure" (Luke 16:7) = 95.78 gallons.

LITRA (Rom. **libra**) translated "pound" (John 12:3) = 13.7 ounces.

METRETES translated "firkin" (John 2:6) = 10.4 gallons.

MODIOS translated "bushel" (Matt. 5:15) = 2.2 gallons.

SATON (seah) translated "measure" (Matt. 13:33) = 3.19 gallons.

XESTES (Rom. sextarius) translated "pot" (Mark 7:4) = 1.15 pints.

For weights large and small balances were used. Weights were mainly of stone. Light ones were carried in wallets. Heavy stone weights were often carved in the shapes of creatures, such as lions and ducks. Pots and jars of various sizes served for measures.

PART VI

LAWS, CUSTOMS, AND BELIEFS

When the Hebrew Bible (the Old Testament) was taking the form in which we now have it, monotheism had finally prevailed as the faith of the Jewish people. It involved belief in One God, eternal, invisible, and omnipotent. But the Bible is witness that this faith had been achieved only after many centuries of spiritual development and a long drawn out struggle with polytheism. Biblical history extends nearly two thousand years when it carries us back to Abraham, the progenitor of the Hebrew race, and punctuates the story with numerous references to the laws, customs and beliefs which were characteristic of the peoples among whom the Hebrews lived at various periods. It was natural to hold that the inhabitants of each land and city had experimental knowledge of the particular divinity under whose protection they dwelt, and whose favors must be solicited in the manner locally appointed as a result of long experience. If a town or territory was conquered it would be folly not to respect the god or goddess of the place, or at least the modes of worship, even if victory had demonstrated the superiority of the divine patron of the victors. The divinity was the real local ruler, whose temple was also his palace, in which he dwelt spiritually, and the priest-king was his son, his servant, and his living embodiment.

The festal seasons were intimately associated with the agricultural year, and the age-old beliefs in the importance of sympathetic magic to assure germination, growth and good harvest, inevitably involved the emphasis of religious sexualism. Of course this pandered to animal instincts and took base forms, and was denounced by those whose concept of God demanded purity and holiness. But its appeal was strong, not only as a welcome mitigation of the drabness and drudgery of the common lot, but to the untutored mind as a logical and indispensable necessity of existence, not to be neglected even when repugnant. The Bible in its final form often applies the standards of a later time to earlier circumstances, and an elevated morality passes harsh judgments on pagan ritual and practices.

Primitive ideas are not easily eradicated, and especially among the peasantry are found to persist in customs and ceremonies, the crude origins of which have long been forgotten or surrendered, or have been given some fresh and more tolerable interpretation. They still lend color to national and community life even in the 20th century, as long after the advent of Jesus Christ as the time of Abraham was before it; and many features of the worship both of the Church and Synagogue preserve notions whose ancestry is in direct conflict with the spiritual and moral philosophy of Judaism and Christianity.

With the New Testament we are in a period when venerable habits and modes of thought were undergoing considerable transformation, receiving new names and expression. Religion was becoming more rationalized and systematic. Among the Jewish masses, angels and demons had replaced the old deities of Canaan—benevolent and malevolent. In the Graeco-Roman world synthesis was busy and the old cults were being allegorized or converted into mysteries. The educated favored various philosophies; but superstition still predominated. There was much greater concern for salvation —the welfare, temporal and eternal, of the individual. The Roman Empire used this concern to maintain its power by creating an Imperial cult, and was challenged by the Jewish and Christian concepts of Theocracy.

The material embraced by the title of this Part of the present work is manifestly far too voluminous and far-reaching to be dealt with other than sketchily and with substantial omissions. We can only illustrate the range and variety of themes by sample, introducing a sufficiency of aspects to convey an impression of what is represented in the biblical records.

ADAD (see **DAD**).

ADONIS. From the semitic **adon** (lord). Greek representation of the god Tammuz, whose death was associated with the summer parching of vegetation. Women planted seeds in bowls, known as **GARDENS OF ADONIS**, which sprouted and quickly withered and were then cast into flowing water with images of the god as a propitiation for the restoration of fertility, perhaps referred to in Isa. 17:9–10. (See also **ASHTORETH, GROVE** and **TAMMUZ.**)

ANGELS, ANGELOLOGY. (Heb. **malachim,** messengers). The heavenly sons of God identified with the spirits of the heavenly bodies, and with phenomena such as lightning and tempest. In the Old Testament God sometimes communicates with men by an Angel of the Lord in human form. In the post-exilic period, partly under the influence of Zoroastrianism, an elaborate angelology developed with both good and bad angels. Choirs of angels continually praise God (Isa. 6; Dan. 7:10). They were later known as the heavenly Watchers. Some of them sinned (Gen. 6:2) and were cast down and imprisoned (II Pet. 2:4). The Essenes were credited with angel-worship. (See also **ARCHANGELS, BELIAL, CHERUBIM AND SERAPHIM, GUARDIAN ANGELS.)**

ANOINTING WITH OIL. In secular usage for refreshment and as a mark of joy; in religious usage an act of consecration. Sacred vessels and objects were anointed, and persons dedicated to God on taking office such as high priests and kings. From this act came the designation Messiah, the anointed one (Greek **Christos**), applied in later times to the ideal high priest and the ideal king. In the New Testament there is reference to anointing the sick in the name of the Lord (Jas. 5:14).

ANTICHRIST. False Messiah. It was a Christian belief that before the Second Advent of Christ a satanic impersonation of him would appear, deceiving the nations and even some of the Elect. He is called the Man of Sin in II Thess. 2:3, and will claim to be divine. Such a claim was made by the Roman emperors, especially Caligula and Domitian. The Imperial regime thus appears as Antichrist in the Revelation.

APHRODITE. Greek goddess akin to the semitic Ashtoreth (Astarte), who mourns the dead Adonis. Identified by the Romans with Venus. The Gardens of Aphrodite were associated with the sacred prostitution of the Fertility Cult. (See also **ASHTORETH**).

ARCHANGELS. A late Jewish concept. The seven chief angels have a relationship to the seven planets and to the seven spirits of God before his throne (Rev. 1:4, 4:5). Their names are Uriel, Raphael, Raguel, Michael, Saraqael, Gabriel and Remiel, according to the Book of Enoch. Only Michael and Gabriel are mentioned by name in the Bible (Dan. 7:16, 10:13; Luke 1:19; Jude 9; Rev. 12:7), and Raphael in the Apocrypha (Tob. 12:15).

ARK OF THE COVENANT. The sacred chest of the Hebrews in which was kept the **TABLES OF THE LAW,** and which was placed in the inmost shrine of the Sanctuary, the Holy of Holies. Such sacred chests were anciently used to house images of the gods, so that when the Israelites brought the Ark into the camp when at war with the Philistines the Philistines thought they had fetched their god (I Sam. 4:7). The Ark was guarded by the effigies of two winged creatures (see **CHERUBIM**).

ARTEMIS. The mother-goddess of Asia who became the Artemis of the Greeks, and was identified with Diana by the Romans because she was the protectress of wild animals. Her principal temple was at Ephesus, one of the wonders of the ancient world. She was depicted with many breasts wearing a robe covered with the heads of animals. The trade in shrines of Artemis was felt to be in jeopardy through Paul's preaching against idolatry at Ephesus (Acts 19).

ASHTORETH (ASTARTE). The semitic goddess who was the consort of Adonis-Tammuz, having a correspondence with Ishtar of the Babylonians and Isis of the Egyptians. She also represented the moon and wore its disk on her head. In this character she was worshipped in Canaan as Ashtoreth-Karnaim (Twin-horned Ashtoreth). Offerings of cakes and incense were made to her as Queen of Heaven (Jer. 44:17–19). As mother-goddess she occupied a central place in the Fertility Cult practiced in the tree plantations dedicated to her (Isa. 1:29, 46:17; Hos. 4:13).

ATONEMENT. Theologically the belief that by repentance, restitution, and expiatory sacrifice, the forgiveness of sins could be procured from God. The Christian form of the doctrine regarded the crucifixion of Jesus as an act of atonement for the sins of mankind, operative while the present world should endure, to assure Divine forgiveness to all who by faith in Jesus availed themselves of the benefit of the sacrifice of himself. Among the Hebrews there had been instituted an annual Day of Atonement, marked by fasting and special rites, the services being led by the high priest who, on this occasion only, entered the Holy of Holies of the Sanctuary. (See also **SCAPEGOAT**).

AZAZEL (see **SCAPEGOAT**).

BAAL. The title of male divinities in Canaan and Syria, meaning master or protector, e.g., Baal-Tarz, patron god of Tarsus. The Baalim (pl.) anciently represented the male principle, symbolized by a monolith or pillar. The Baal was in one aspect the sun god as Ashtoreth was the moon goddess.

BAPTISM. Ritual washing or bathing as a means of purification both physical and spiritual. Uncleanness was associated with menstruation and child-birth, certain diseases, contact with a corpse, idolatry, etc. Thus converts from heathenism were baptized. The bathing pool was essential to the purity required by the Essenes, and John the Baptist employed the rite to signify repentance from the defilement of being astray from God, outside the company of the Elect. The rite had a similar significance in Christianity, and the dipping in water linked the believer with the burial and resurrection of Christ.

BAPTISTS. In New Testament times the sect of followers of John the Baptist, who held the belief that he was the Priestly Messiah.

BAR-MITZVAH. The term means 'son of the commandment' and marks the attainment by a Jewish boy of his spiritual majority at the age of thirteen, when he becomes responsible in Jewish law for the sins he commits. On attaining this majority he joins in worship as an adult member of the congregation.

BAT-QOL (Daughter of a Voice). In biblical times it was believed that a message from God might be received by an inner awareness of words or ideas (I Kings 19:12; Matt. 3:17), by the providential overhearing of something said by someone which gave illumination or guidance, or by interpreting in language some external sound such as a roll of thunder (Exod. 20:19; John 12:28–29). It was only when the direct Voice of God was regarded by the Jews as having ceased because of the sins of the people that the bat-qol came to be thought of as a kind of secondary substitute.

BELIAL. In the Old Testament a worthless person; "man of belial" or "son of belial" (Judg. 19:22; I Sam. 25:25). In later times Belial, like Satan, was used as a designation of the Evil One, the angelic power opposed to the purposes of God (II Cor. 6:15).

BENEDICTIONS. In post-exilic Judaism it became customary to formulate set blessings to accompany the performance of ceremonial acts and as addenda to prayer in doxologies. Such blessings were also devised by the Pharisees in language appropriate to a great variety of experiences in daily life (e.g. Matt. 9:8). The practice was followed in Christian doxologies. In ancient times the priests were charged with blessing the people in the name of God (Num. 6:23–27). It was a delightful custom to bless children, accompanying the words with laying hands on their heads (Mark 10:16).

BINDING AND LOOSING. The power of religious authorities to forbid or permit practices derived by interpretation from the Mosaic Law. This power was claimed by leading Pharisees and conferred by Jesus on his disciples (Matt. 16:19).

BITTER HERBS (see **PASSOVER**).

BLOOD. Blood was regarded as the vehicle of life. Among the Hebrews, therefore, the eating of flesh with the blood in it was forbidden, as it was among the early Christians (Acts 15:20).

BLUE THREAD. The Hebrews were required to insert a blue thread in the fringe on their garments as a reminder of God's commandments (Num. 15:38, and see further under **FRINGED GARMENT**).

BOOK OF LIFE. It was an ancient belief that the names and deeds of the righteous were recorded in heaven. This was not peculiar to the Hebrews. Later the Book of Life was associated with the final Day of Judgment (Dan. 12:1; Rev. 20:12).

BOOTH (see **TABERNACLES**).

BREAD AND WINE SANCTIFICATION (see **KIDDUSH**).

CAKES OFFERED TO THE QUEEN OF HEAVEN (see **ASHTORETH**).

CALF, GOLDEN. The Israelites at Sinai turned to the worship of a golden bullock (Exod. 32), and similar images were set up by Jeroboam, king of Israel, at Dan and Bethel (I Kings 12:28–29). These were probably similar to representations of the Egyptian god Apis.

CHASSIDIM (The Pious). Name of a movement about the beginning of the 2nd century B.C. which contended for strict adherence to the Jewish faith in opposition to Hellenic influences. The movement appears to have originated among the priests, but included many laymen. It gave rise to the Pharisees and especially the Essenes.

CHEMOSH. Chief god of the Moabites. On the stele of Mesha, king of Moab, the god's activities are described in terms similar to those used by the Jews of Yahweh.

CHERUBIM AND SERAPHIM. Mythological creatures representative of the forces of Nature, attendant upon God and acting as the heavenly transporters of his throne. The Cherubim were four-winged and the Seraphim six-winged. Representations of the Cherubim guarded the Ark of the Covenant. Theophanies in which these creatures appear occur in Isa. 6 and Ezek. 10. Similar concepts are found in Egypt and Babylon.

CHOSEN PEOPLE. The belief of the Hebrews that they were a people dedicated to the service of God as a priestly nation. Israel was set apart among the nations as the tribe of Levi was set apart as the priestly tribe in Israel. The early Christians thought of themselves as inheriting the place of the Chosen People as the ultimate Israel (I Pet. 2:9).

CIRCUMCISION. The cutting away of the foreskin, a rite practiced widely in ancient Egypt and other countries of the Middle East. Among the Hebrews the operation was performed on male children on the eighth day from birth and associated with the Covenant made by God with Abraham (Gen. 17).

CITIES OF REFUGE. The Israelites set aside six cities, three on each side of the Jordan, as Cities of Refuge to which persons guilty of unintentional manslaughter could flee and escape the vengeance of the dead man's family. The refugee had to remain in the city until the death of the contemporary high priest, when he was free to leave with impunity (Num. 35).

CONTACT WITH A CORPSE. In Hebrew law this rendered a person unclean. Such contact was forbidden to high priests and those under a Nazirite vow even in the case of close relations (Lev. 21:11; Num. 6:5).

CORBAN. Offering made to God in discharge of a vow. Later the term covered votary gifts of all kinds, and such gifts formed part of the sacred treasure of the Temple. The Roman governor Pontius Pilate seized the Corban to build an aqueduct to bring water to Jerusalem, which provoked a rising. A reference to the misuse of the principle of corban is given in Mark 7:11.

COVENANT. The making of a binding compact for any purpose, anciently sealed by a sacrifice to mark its solemnity. In the Bible there is reference to a number of Covenants made by God with men, such as the Covenant with Noah, the Covenant with the Patriarchs, the Covenant with Israel at Sinai, the Covenant with the tribe of Levi, and the Covenant with the house of David. The death of Jesus was accepted by Christians as the sealing of a New Covenant in His blood.

CREATION. Compared with ancient concepts of the Creation prevailing in the Middle East, that of the Bible is simple and elevated in tone. The visible universe proceeds from the invisible God, and on earth man is made in God's image as the expression of the mysterious projection of the unseen into the seen. According to the New Testament (Col. 1), Christ was that projection, and therefore the beginning of creation. There was a Jewish belief that the angels were created on the first of the six days of Creation.

DAD (ADAD). Syrian god resembling the Babylonian Tammuz and therefore associated with the Fertility Cult, whose death was mourned with the drying up of vegetation in the summer. The name is also found combined with that of Ramman the storm god (Hadad-Rimmon, Zech. 12:11).

DANCING, RELIGIOUS. Rhythmic dancing by troops of men and maidens, not in combination of the sexes, was a feature of ancient worship, especially connected with agriculture and therefore with the Fertility Cult. Dancing in the vineyards was a venerable custom (Judg. 21:21), still followed in August and October in the time of Christ, when young men would choose their brides. On these occasions the girls dressed in white. In II Sam. 6:14 there is reference to David dancing before the Ark.

DECALOGUE. The basic moral and religious code of the Hebrews was set down in Ten Commandments said to have been delivered by God to Moses on Mt. Sinai, engraved on two tables of stone. It was customary in the ancient world to hold that the Laws were given by God to the king (e.g., the Code of Hammurabi).

DEMONS. The belief in harmful spirits of various kinds goes back to the very dawn of religion. Babylonian influences were largely responsible for the demonology of Judaism prevalent in the time of Christ. Popular belief peopled gloomy gorges and waste places with malignant spirits, and regarded many forms of disease and sickness as due to demonic possession. Charms and amulets were worn to give protection, and rites and incantations were employed to exorcise the demons. In the Gospels there are many accounts of Jesus casting out evil spirits, and conferring the power to do so on his followers.

DEVIL (see **SATAN**).

DIETARY LAWS. The Laws of Moses distinguished between clean and unclean animals (see Part II, Natural History). Only the clean might be eaten. The Food Laws served both a hygienic purpose and as a counter to idolatrous practices. Israel was to be a holy nation. In keeping with this conception the Jews washed their hands before touching their food and kept all utensils clean (Mark 7:4).

DIVINATION. The consultation of deity for guidance followed a great variety of methods in the ancient world, conducted by the priests and by those who made a profession of the occult arts. Some of these methods relied on chance. Others embraced astrology, necromancy, and the interpretation of dreams. Less familiar are divination with arrows and looking at the entrails or liver of a sacrificed animal (Ezek. 21:21), divination by rods (Hos. 4:12), divination from the flight of birds, and among the Israelites, oracular consultation of Urim and Thummim, which were kept behind the breastplate of the high priest and may have been some kind of stones representing positive and negative responses.

DIVINITY OF KINGS. In the olden days kings, like priests, were sacred persons having received anointing as such. They were the visible representatives of the national god, therefore sons of God, being accorded divine honors. Aspects of this belief prevailed among the Hebrews, but neither their kings nor priests were treated as gods, an idea repugnant to their monotheism. (See also **EMPEROR CULT**).

DUALISM. The belief in opposing Powers of Good and Evil entered into the ancient religions, dualism being developed by the Persians in the doctrine of Ahura-Mazda and Ahriman. This concept influenced eclectic Judaism as represented by the Essenes and early Christians in doctrines of the Two Spirits, the Two Ways, Christ and Antichrist. The Pharisees endorsed the idea of the Good Inclination and the Evil Inclination in man. But such ideas among the Jews were not allowed to detract from faith in One God.

EL (pl. **ELOHIM**). The semitic word for God in the Bible, employed also by other semites, to denote in the singular "a god" and in the plural "deity." For the Israelites the compound Yahweh-Elohim (rendered "Lord God") signified Yahweh the supreme Deity.

ELECTION. The beginnings of the doctrine of Election found in the New Testament go back to the Old Testament concept of a Chosen People represented latterly by a remnant loyal to God and his laws. The doctrine as developed by Chassidic Judaism and in Christianity argued that the faithful Remnant of the Last Days had been chosen and foreordained by God and thus were the Elect. The Messiah (Christ) was himself the Elect One.

EMPEROR CULT. The Roman emperors, from the time of Augustus, accepted from the east the belief in the divinity of kings. Consequently they bore divine titles, being regarded and worshipped as Son of God, Jupiter incarnate. Temples to the god Augustus and the goddess Roma were established in the Roman provinces. Belief in imperial apotheosis proved a useful instrument of political policy to keep subject peoples loyal to Rome. The Jews were exempted from emperor worship, but not the Christians, who were regarded as subversive as setting up in Jesus a rival divine emperor. They suffered martyrdom for refusing to offer sacrifice and burn incense before the emperor's image.

EPICUREANS. Paul in Athens encountered adherents of this philosophy. Its founder was Epicurus, born in Samos in 341 B.C. His followers bought him a house and garden in Athens, where he taught from 306. The school was more concerned with the science of living than with speculation about the universe, and got the reputation of indulging in escapism and being pleasure-loving. But the essence of Epicureanism was that people should be happy and at peace with themselves under all conditions, not chasing after the good, but adhering to ways and principles that brought contentment and created bonds of sympathetic and understanding friendship.

ESSENES. A Jewish religious order which emerged in the 2nd century B.C. from Chassidism. The Essenes believed themselves to be called apart, the more diligently to pursue the study and practice of the Laws of God in evil times, and to represent the forces of Light in the final struggle with the forces of Darkness. They had a reputation for knowing many secrets of nature, for healing and foretelling the future. To become a full member of their order required a long and strenuous novitiate. A much clearer picture of their ideas and discipline has been obtained from their literature found at their center near the Dead Sea, the texts known as the Dead Sea Scrolls. Primitive Christianity was in certain things indebted to the Essenes.

EXORCISM. The art of freeing human beings from possession by demons or other inimical spiritual forces regarded as the cause of some forms of insanity, disease and sickness. A great variety of methods were employed involving the pronouncement of magical words, the performance of ritual actions, and medical treatment. The early Christians used the name of Jesus as a word of power to cast out demons.

FALL OF MAN. The doctrine that by the sin of Adam (the first man in the Bible) all mankind came under the power of sin and consequently became liable to death. Jewish teaching accepted that there was a disposition to sin in all men, but held that this could be overcome by each individual through obedience to the commandments of God. Christian teaching, as set out by St. Paul, made all men share the sin of Adam from which they could only be released by faith in the atoning work of Jesus Christ the second Adam from heaven. (See further under **ATONEMENT, REDEMPTION**).

FASTING. Voluntarily going without food was called by the Hebrews "afflicting the soul" and was followed as a mark of mourning and to express contrition for sin. The Day of

Atonement was instituted as an annual obligatory fast day for sin.

FIRSTBORN, REDEMPTION OF. By a venerable custom the male firstborn of man and beast belonged to God. In Exod. 13 this custom is related to the redemption from Egypt. By a law, the tribe of Levi and the cattle of the Levites were dedicated to God in substitution for the firstborn of man and beast among the other tribes of Israel (Num. 3). But since the numbers of the firstborn exceeded the total of Levites the excess were redeemed by a payment to the Levitical priesthood of five shekels. This applied to unclean beasts as well as human beings. The firstlings of clean cattle were offered as sacrifices (Num. 18). The priests and Levites and their cattle, as already dedicated, did not require to be redeemed. In New Testament times all Jews made the monetary payment for their male firstborn (Luke 2:23).

FIRSTFRUITS. As with the firstborn, the firstfruits of the land were offered to God at Jerusalem, those of the first two years of each seven-year cycle being eaten at the festivals and of the third year distributed as charity. Later a tithing system came into operation in respect of firstfruits. The offering of the firstfruits of produce was associated with the three Pilgrim Feasts, Passover (barley), Pentecost (wheat), and Tabernacles (fruit).

FLOOD. The biblical story of the Flood has utilized for religious teaching traditions of a great catastrophe which occurred in the early dawn of historical times. The Babylonian Gilgamesh Epic contains a comparable Sumerian tradition of a Mesopotamian deluge, the hero Utnapishtim answering in certain respects to the Biblical Noah. Excavations at Ur have helped, by revealing a mud deposit beneath which were indications of an earlier civilization, to date the catastrophe which may be reflected in both traditions at about 4000 B.C.

FRINGED GARMENT. The woolen garment of the ancient east had a fringed edge, in which the Israelites were required to insert a blue thread to remind them of the divine commandments. In conformity with this law the Jews continued to wear a fringed robe or cloak containing the thread, which explains the Gospel references to the "hem of the garment" of Jesus (Matt. 9:29). The Pharisees enlarged these fringes (Matt. 23:5).

GEHENNA. Aramaic form of the Hebrew Gehinnom (Valley of Hinnom) otherwise called Tophet. This valley outside Jerusalem was notorious because here children had of old been burnt as sacrifices to Moloch, and the place appears later to have been used for burning refuse. Thus its name came to symbolize the place of punishment of the wicked by fiery torment, just as the Garden of Eden came to symbolize the place of bliss of the righteous. Both ideas were figurative.

GLEANING FIELDS. The Law of Moses required the Hebrews not to reap the corners of their fields, nor to glean after the harvesting of grain and fruit. The gleanings were to be left for the benefit of widows, orphans and strangers (Lev. 19:9; Deut. 24:20; Ruth 2:2).

GRACE OF GOD. The exercise by God of the divine prerogative of mercy towards human beings who have violated his laws, since he is a loving and long suffering Father as well as the supreme Judge. St. Paul set out a doctrine of Grace, by which this gift of God's favor was secured by faith in the atoning death of Jesus Christ.

GROVE (Asherah). Single trees or groups of trees, notably the oak and tamarisk, also posts set up in imitation of trees, signifying the presence of a deity and therefore representing a sacred site, having a particular relationship to the Fertility Cult.

GUARDIAN ANGELS. A late belief in the existence of heavenly representatives of persons and peoples. Michael is the angelic prince of Israel in Dan. 10, where reference is also made to the angel princes of Persia and Greece. The angels of children are mentioned in Matt. 18:10, the angels of churches in Rev. 1:20, and the angel of Jesus in Rev. 22:16.

HERMES. In Greek mythology the divine messenger of the gods answering to the Roman Mercury (Acts 14:12).

HIGH PLACES. Associated with pagan worship. High Places were not confined to natural eminences like mountains and hills, and might be set up on low ground by building an altar approached by steps.

HORNS OF THE ALTAR. Projections at the corners of the altar. Taking hold of the horns of the altar was a way of obtaining sanctuary (I Kings 1:50, 2:28).

HUMAN SACRIFICE. The sacrifice of children, especially the firstborn, was practiced in ancient times as a means of propitiating the gods, particularly when danger threatened. The Law of Moses denounces the sacrifice of children as burnt offerings to Moloch (Lev. 18:21, 20:2), and the same repudiation is implicit in the account of the offering of Isaac in Gen. 22. The sacrifice of children at the building of cities, when the bodies were placed in the foundations, is referred to in I Kings 16:34.

INCARNATION. The dwelling of a divine being in a human body, an idea common in antiquity. Kings were anciently regarded as incarnating the national deity. Christian doctrine holds that Jesus Christ was the incarnation of the Word of God, the Son of God, or first expression of the invisible Godhead, and is also related to the divinity of kings through the conception of the Messiah. (See also **LOGOS**).

INCENSE. Perfumes which gave sensual pleasure and refreshment have always been prized in the east, and regarded therefore as pleasing to the gods. But the burning of incense in worship also symbolized the ascension of prayer to heaven because the smoke rose up in a straight column (Ps. 141:2; Rev. 8:4).

ISHTAR (see **ASHTORETH**).

JUBILEE. Under the Law of Moses every seventh year was a Sabbatic Year for the land. Sowing and pruning were forbidden. Produce growing of its own accord was not to be harvested. After every 49 years the fiftieth year was a Jubilee Year heralded by trumpets, when all bondservants had to be released and real estate returned to its ancestral owners (Lev. 25).

JUDGMENT IN THE GATE. It was the ancient custom to deal with civil causes in the open space inside the entrance of the city gate, which was the place of meetings of the elders of the city. Kings would also sit in the gate to administer justice (Deut. 22:15; Ruth 4:1; II Sam. 15:2, 19:8; Prov. 31:23).

KIDDUSH. The sanctification of bread and wine by the recital of a blessing for each, customary on Sabbaths and festivals, these products symbolizing God's care for his creatures. The ceremony was performed by Jesus at the Last Supper.

KINGDOM OF GOD. The Messianic Era when God will be acknowledged by all mankind as Supreme Ruler of the world. The time of the advent of Jesus Christ was regarded by many as heralding the establishment of the final Theocracy.

LEVIRATE MARRIAGE. The Law of Moses provided that if a man died childless his brother or male next of kin should marry the widow, the firstborn of the second marriage succeeding to the name of the deceased (Deut. 25; Matt. 22:24). If a man refused this obligation the ancient custom was that the widow took off his shoe and spat in his face in presence of the elders.

LOGOS. The Greek term is variously used for word, theme, reason, and was employed in the 1st century A.D. by the Jewish philosopher Philo of Alexandria to represent the eternal Mind or Wisdom of God made manifest in creation. The Logos is personified as Son of God. St. Paul equated God's revelation of himself in the visible universe with the Jewish concept of the pre-existent Messiah and Primordial Heavenly Man, identifying Jesus Christ with this concept as the first projection of the invisible Godhead, the scheme or image of Himself on which the whole universe was framed. The prologue to the Fourth Gospel describes the incarnation of the Logos in the person of Jesus.

MAGI. In origin an Iranian priestly order of wise men, soothsayers and astrologers, similar to the Hindu Brahmin. Later the name was applied to any sage, especially eastern, claiming knowledge of the ancient wisdom and the exercise of occult powers. In Matthew's account of the birth of Jesus magi come to Jerusalem, having learnt from a celestial phenomenon that a king of the Jews has been born. Similar stories are told in Jewish legend of the nativities of Abraham and Moses in which such magi play a part.

MANDRAKE. Eating mandrake pulled from the ground was held to assist fertility in human beings. Hence the name "Love Apples" (Gen. 30:14).

MARDUK. The Mesopotamian hero-god, who cut in two Tiamat (primordial substance) and thereby formed heaven and earth. He was the creator of mankind and ruler of human destiny, divine lord of the world.

MESSIAH. The ancient custom of consecrating high priests and kings by anointing with oil led to the description of such persons as "anointed ones" (messiahs). The perpetual covenants with the house of Levi and the house of David gave rise to the doctrine of an ultimate ideal high priest and king, a Priestly and a Davidic Messiah, regarded by some, like the Essenes, as a distinct person. A mystical view thought of the Messiah as having existed in heaven, of having been designated, from the beginning of Creation ready for his manifestation in the Last Time (see **LOGOS**). The Pharisees seem to have regarded him as performing a temporary function in overcoming the enemies of Israel and inaugurating the Kingdom of God. He would be heralded by the priestly prophet Elijah returned from heaven. Jewish thought also entertained the idea of a Suffering Messiah. But the appearance of the Messiah or Messiahs is always connected with the climax of human history, and there was no clear and settled teaching on the subject. The foundation of Christianity was the belief that Jesus was the Messiah (Gr. **Christos**).

MILLENNARIANISM. The eschatological view that the Messianic Age would endure for a thousand years. This would be the Sabbatical seventh millennium from the date of the Creation, a concept partly derived from Iranian-Babylonian thought. In the early Christian Church it was believed that Jesus would return from heaven to rule the world for a thousand years in association with the resurrected righteous. After this would come the Last Judgment.

MITHRAISM. A religion which blended worship of the Iranian sun-god Mithras with the Fertility Cult, producing a mystery faith relating to death and resurrection, in which only men could be initiated. Mithras had been miraculously born, and had killed the bull whose blood gave life to the world. He underwent death and rebirth. The rites of Mithras were conducted in caves or crypts beneath his temple, where initiates were bathed in the blood of a sacrificed bull as a purification from sin and entrance into newness of life. Mithraism had a Lord's Day in Sunday, a sacrament of bread and wine, and in so many ways resembled Christianity that it was regarded by the Church as a diabolical substitute invented to deceive mankind.

MONOTHEISM. The belief in one sole God which became the religion of the Jews. It excluded the recognition or worship of any other god and repudiated all idolatry and representation of the Deity. Earlier Yahweh had been regarded as the God of Israel and the Supreme God, Most High God.

MOURNING RITES. The actions dictated were those in direct contrast to the expression of joy, and included tearing of garments and gashing the body, wearing sackcloth, shaving the head and beard, putting dust and ashes on the head and sitting on the ground, while women wailed and dirges were played on musical instruments. Some of these customs (Jer. 16:6–8) were still practiced in the time of Christ, while others had been modified or abolished.

MUTILATION. Religious frenzy in ancient pagan faiths caused the priests to gash themselves with knives (I Kings 18:28), and devotees even castrated themselves.

NEBO. Popular Mesopotamian deity, similar to Hermes as the messenger and interpreter of the gods. He was regarded as the son of Bel-Marduk, and his name enters into many personal names like Nabopolasser and Nabonidus.

NAZIRITE, NAZARITE. A person consecrated to God by a vow either temporarily or permanently. Such persons might not partake of anything connected with the vine, or any intoxicant, and might not cut their hair. They must conduct themselves as if they were priests. Lifelong Nazirites were the prophet Samuel and John the Baptist. The law of the Nazirite is given in Num. 6:1–21.

PARADISE. The biblical story of the Garden of Eden appears to have had its origin in Egyptian ideas of the Fields of the Blessed, and a number of Egyptian associations can be traced in the description. Egyptian men were depicted as red-skinned, and the Hebrew name for man, Adam, has the same significance. The earthly Paradise, like the land of Egypt, was watered by a river (Gen. 13:10). Later Jewish thought gave the name of the Garden of Eden or Paradise to the place of eternal felicity of the righteous.

PASSOVER. The spring festival associated with the exodus from Egypt. The festival commenced with the slaying of the paschal lamb on the 14th of the month Nisan, one lamb for each household, to be roasted whole and eaten with unleavened bread and bitter herbs, while the story of the deliverance from bondage was recited. All leaven had to be destroyed, and the Feast of Unleavened Bread was kept for seven days. By the time of Christ there had developed an elaborate domestic ritual for the eve of the Passover which is represented in the Gospels by the Last Supper.

PENTECOST. The Feast of Weeks, second of the Pilgrim Festivals when Jews went up to Jerusalem. It was observed seven weeks after Passover on the 6th of the month Sivan, marking the end of the grain harvest when the first fruits of wheat were offered. The festival became identified with the Giving of the Law on Sinai and among Christians with the outpouring of the Holy Spirit.

PHARISEES. The fellowship of laymen dedicated to the strict observance of the Mosaic Law and originating in the 2nd century B.C. The Hebrew name Perushim, meaning "those who separate," may have been connected with the law of separating the sacred tithe, but came to be regarded as keeping separate from sinners. Though their number was small they had great influence with the people for their purity, piety and championship of national independence, and played an important part in political affairs. The Pharisees laid the foundations of orthodox Judaism.

PHYLACTERIES. Small leather boxes containing passages from the Pentateuch written on parchment, namely Exod. 13:2–16; Deut. 6:4–9, 13–23, worn on the forehead and upper left arm during morning prayer, except on Sabbaths and holy days. They represented, literally, "the sign upon thy hand and frontlets between thine eyes" (Deut. 6:8). The boxes were attached by leather straps. Phylactery is from the Greek, meaning amulet. The Jews called them Tefillin (prayers) because used at the time of morning prayer. The practice probably originated with the Pharisees (Matt. 23:5), and does not seem to have been general among Jews at the time of Christ.

POSTURES IN PRAYER. (1) **Adoration,** standing with both arms uplifted and the hands level with the face, palms outward, (2) **Supplication,** standing or kneeling with eyes lifted and hands outstretched level with the shoulders, with the palms upward, (3) **Worship,** prostrating with knees bent and head and hands touching the ground.

PROSTITUTION, SACRED. This was associated with the ancient Fertility Cult, both male and female prostitutes being attached to the temples as servants of the god or goddess. Such sacred men and sacred women were to be found at the

Temple of Jerusalem when polytheism predominated (I Kings 15:12; II Kings 23:7).

PYTHONIC SPIRIT. Oracular ventriloquial utterance held to be inspired by the Pythian Apollo. Python was the serpent guarding the oracle at Delphi, killed by the god Apollo who inherited the oracle. A slave girl with the pythonic gift, possessed by the spirit, is mentioned in Acts 16:16–18.

QUEEN OF HEAVEN (see **ASHTORETH**).

REDEMPTION. The action of buying back, ransoming, delivering from bondage, effecting release. God is the Redeemer of his people from captivity by achieving their freedom and restoration. He also redeems the individual from sin and death. In the New Testament Jesus, by shedding his blood, is God's agent of redemption. Those who accept his sacrifice are in this sense persons who have been purchased or ransomed.

RESURRECTION. Restoration to life from the state of death by the physical reanimation of the individual. Late Jewish belief developed a doctrine of a general resurrection in the Last Times, though by no means all Jews accepted it. Christians held that believers in Jesus would be resurrected at his second advent at the commencement of the Messianic Era, while the rest of mankind would be resurrected at its termination. Those judged unworthy of immortality would then suffer a second death. Persons raised at the return of Christ, and those living at that time, would be given a body not subject to decay. Jesus, when raised by God from the dead, had been the first to receive such a body, becoming therefore "the firstfruits of them that sleep."

RIGHTEOUSNESS. For Hebrews living in accordance with the commandments of God as laid down in the Law of Moses. Violation of the Law was sin, and righteousness must be regained by repentance and atonement. The non-Jew was regarded as in a state of sin because of idolatry, but Judaism taught that Gentiles qualified as righteous by obedience to the requirements of the Primeval Law, or seven Laws of Noah, of which those listed in Acts 15:29 are typical. St. Paul held that the perfect righteousness of Christ served for all who should have faith in him, and such righteousness could not be achieved otherwise, since it was impossible for the ordinary individual to keep the whole Law.

SACRIFICE OF CHILDREN (see **HUMAN SACRIFICE**).

SADDUCEES. Party among the Jews drawing adherents chiefly from the hierarchy and upper class, representing more literally traditional Hebrew teaching of the theocratic government vested in the descendants of Zadok, high priest in the reign of Solomon. In the 2nd century B.C. the Maccabees took the high priesthood from the Zadokites (Sadducees), but these continued to play a prominent part in government, and opposed the ideas of the Pharisees. Popularly, the Sadducees were disliked as favoring foreign ways and as subservient to the Romans.

SALVATION. Deliverance from peril and continuance in a state of security and wellbeing, frequently by divine intervention. The idea of savior gods is very ancient, and such salvation was credited to the Roman emperor in the Emperor Cult. Among the Jews the term came to be applied to deliverance from the ultimate penalties, salvation from the Wrath to Come. For Christians salvation was obtained through Jesus Christ, the saved person by continuing in faith being entitled to share in the first resurrection, receiving immortality and sharing in the bliss of the Messianic Era.

SATAN. The word means adversary, and as a personal name is applied in the Old Testament to the celestial being who accuses men to God. Later Satan was regarded as hostile to man, tempting men to disobey God, and identified with the serpent in Genesis who tempted Eve. For the faithful he became the archangelic rebel against God, leader of the hosts of darkness and ruler of the present sinful world order.

SCAPEGOAT. Goat which symbolically carried away the sins of the people (Lev. 16). Two goats were selected for the Day of Atonement, one for the Lord sacrificed as a sin-offering for the high priest and his household, and the other for Azazel, possibly an elemental spirit of the wilderness. The second goat was released alive into the wilderness as scapegoat. In the time of Christ the scapegoat had its horns bound with a scarlet thread, and appears to have been killed in the wilderness by hurling it from a cliff, when according to legend the thread of scarlet turned white with reference to Isa. 1:18.

SECOND ADVENT. The Christian belief that in the Last Times Jesus Christ, who had ascended to heaven after his resurrection, would return to earth to judge the nations, confer immortality on the saints, and reign over the world in glory throughout the millennium.

SHAMASH. The semitic sun god, the moon god being called Sin.

SHEOL. Hebrew for the grave. In later times signifying the underworld of the dead similar to the Greek Hades (Hell).

SHOES, REMOVAL OF. It was customary to take off the shoes before treading on holy ground (Exod. 3:5). The custom is retained by Moslems and Samaritans. (For another shoe custom see under **LEVIRATE MARRIAGE**).

SOUL. Heb. **nephesh** (breath). Soul distinguishes the animate from the inanimate. The soul came to be regarded as the pure personality entering the body at birth and withdrawn at death. During life it could be contaminated by sin, and would be judged with the body at the resurrection. The Hebraic belief was opposed to the Greek idea that the body was the prison house of the soul, a conception developed in Gnostic dualism.

SPEAKING WITH TONGUES. A form of ecstatic utterance, not necessarily in any human language. It was a common manifestation in the early Christian communities.

STOICS. Followers of a Greek philosophy taking its name from the **stoa** (colonnades) of the market at Athens where this school of thought met. Stoicism was founded by Zeno, and taught that men should cultivate moral virtue and be masters of themselves in whatever circumstances they were placed. Whatever befell should be accepted with dignity and borne with fortitude. What mattered was not the pursuit of happiness, but growth in grace. Stoicism touched Pauline Christianity at many points, particularly in the teaching of the Roman Stoic Seneca.

TABERNACLES. Feast of Booths marking the ingathering of the fruit harvest celebrated for seven days in the seventh month Tishri (Lev. 23:39–43). The festival was accompanied by the manifestations of joy. For seven days each family dwelt in a booth open to the sky, having made the pilgrimage to Jerusalem. The worshippers carried into the Temple palm branches bound with myrtle and willow of the brook, and also a citron (**ethrog**). The branches called **lulab** were waved daily towards the altar. Water brought from the Pool of Siloam was poured by the officiating priests into a funnel of the altar as well as the wine offering. At the end of the festival came the Eighth Day of Solemn Assembly, or Great Hosanna (John 7:37). On this day the priests made a sevenfold circuit of the altar chanting from Ps. 118, finally beating their branches against it to denude them of leaves. In the evenings there was dancing with torches.

TAMMUZ. The semitic "divine shepherd" whose death by the goring of a wild boar symbolized the summer drying up of vegetation. Mourning for him was an annual rite (Ezek. 8:14). The goddess Ishtar, his lover, descended into the underworld to bring him back; his resurrection signifying the revival of plant life. (See **ADONIS** and **ASHTORETH**).

TERAPHIM. Images of the gods kept in homes for family protection, first mentioned in the Bible in Gen. 31:19. They could be quite small, or large as in I Sam. 19:13. Such figures, often quite crude, may reflect an earlier ancestor worship. It is possible that in early times images of Yahweh were made (Judg. 17:4–5). The law against graven images was clearly not obeyed in the letter until post-exilic times.

TITHE. The venerable custom of dedicating to God the tenth of produce or possessions as an expression of thanksgiving (Gen. 14:20, 28:20–22). The Hebrew laws of tithing are found in Lev. 27:30–33; Num. 18:21–26; Deut. 14:22–29. Under the monarchy we find a system of tithing as a state tax (I Sam. 8:15–17), but this may have operated only in the reign of Solomon. (See also **FIRSTFRUITS**).

TREE OF LIFE. The tree in the Garden of Eden, the fruit of which conferred immortality (Gen. 3:22–24). In Rev. 22:2 the tree appears in the New Jerusalem, based on Ezek. 47:12. The concept has associations with the ancient Tree Cult, and the sacred tree of life, food and health seems to have been identified with the bisexual date palm.

URIM AND THUMMIM (see **DIVINATION**).

PART VII

NOTABLE NAMES (A-K)

In this Part, and Part VIII, brief but useful information is given about a number of biblical personalities and certain others who feature in contemporary history, and whose lives in many cases have a bearing on biblical events and religious thought. Inevitably the names of a great many individuals have been omitted, but the endeavor has been made to provide a list which is representative to the extent that some of those included may be unfamiliar to the general reader.

AARON. First high priest of Israel (Exod. 28). He was of the tribe of Levi, born in Egypt to Amram and Jochebed, having an elder sister Miriam and a younger brother Moses (Exod. 7:7). In seeking release of the Israelites from Egypt he acted as spokesman for Moses in interviews with Pharaoh. At Sinai, while Moses was on the mount, he yielded to the people in making a golden calf (Exod. 32). Confirmed in the high priesthood (Num. 17), he, like Moses, was not allowed to enter the Promised Land and died on Mt. Hor (Num. 20). By Elisheba he had four sons, Nadab, Abihu, Eleazar and Ithamar. The first two predeceased him (Lev. 10:1–2) and he was succeeded as high priest by Eleazar.

ABEL. Son of Adam and Eve. He had an elder brother Cain. Abel was a shepherd while Cain tilled the soil. When both made offerings to God, that of Abel was accepted and Cain killed him out of jealousy (Gen. 4). First martyred righteous man (Matt. 23:35).

ABIATHAR. Son of Ahimelech, 11th high priest (line of Ithamar). He escaped the massacre of the priests at Nob by Saul, king of Israel, and joined David (I Sam. 22). He officiated during the reign of David with Zadok (line of Eleazar). Finally implicated in the revolt of Adonijah, he was deprived of office in favor of Zadok and banished by Solomon (I Kings 1–2).

ABIGAIL. Famed for her beauty and sense. Married David after the death of her husband Nabal (I Sam. 25), and bore him a son Chileab (II Sam. 3:3).

ABIJAM (ABIJAH). King of Judah, son of Rehoboam and grandson of Solomon. Waged war with Jeroboam I, king of Israel (I Kings 15).

ABIMELECH (1) Son of Gideon (Jerubbaal), made ruler of Israel at Shechem after massacring his brothers, only Jotham escaping. His exploits and death are recorded in Judg. 9. (2) Kings of Gerar in the time of Abraham and Isaac (Gen. 21, 26).

ABINADAB (1) Housed the Ark of the Covenant at Kirjath-jearim when it was returned by the Philistines (I Sam. 7). (2) A son of Saul, killed with his father at the Battle of Mt. Gilboa (I Sam. 31:2).

ABISHAI. Nephew of David and brother of his commander Joab. Loyal to David and rated a hero for his exploits, but merciless (I Sam. 26:6; II Sam. 3:30, 21, 23, etc.).

ABNER. Cousin of King Saul and captain of his army. He made Saul's son Ishbosheth king of Israel, but came over to the side of David. He was killed out of revenge and jealousy by Joab, David's general (II Sam. 2–3).

ABRAHAM (ABRAM). Founder of the Hebrew nation. Born in Ur of the Chaldees in the first half of the 2nd millennium B.C., son of Terah, married to Sarai (Sarah). The family removed to Haran in northern Mesopotamia and afterwards Abraham, taking with him his nephew Lot, migrated to Canaan. He had a son Ishmael by Sarah's Egyptian maid Hagar at Sarah's request, and then Isaac by Sarah herself in old age. Abraham was the recipient of divine promises and the covenant of circumcision (Gen. 11–25).

ABSALOM. Son of David noted for his physical beauty. He led a revolt to seize the throne and forced David into exile. Finally he was defeated and killed by David's general Joab (II Sam. 13–19).

ADAD-'IDRI (HADADEZER). Powerful Aramaean king who with his allies contended with Shalmaneser, king of Assyria, at the Battle of Qarqar (853 B.C.). One of the allies was Ahab, king of Israel, formerly in conflict with Adad-'Idri's father, Benhadad (I Kings 20), and subsequently probably with Adad-'Idri himself, losing his life in battle with the Syrians (I Kings 22).

ADAM. Progenitor of the race which gave rise to the peoples of biblical history and through one line to the Israelites. Married to Eve and father of sons Cain, Abel, and Seth. Originally lived with Eve in the Paradise of Eden, expelled for disobedience to God's commandments. His divine creation and subsequent story is told in Gen. 2–4, and its theological significance in the New Testament is dealt with in the epistles of St. Paul, notably in Rom. 5 and I Cor. 15.

ADONIJAH. One of the sons of David who hoped to succeed his father, who, however, had his son Solomon by Bathsheba proclaimed king. Adonijah's attempt to obtain the throne was thwarted, but his life was spared. His later intrigues caused Solomon to order his execution (I Kings 1–2).

AGABUS. A Jewish disciple of Jesus with the gift of prophecy (Acts 11:28, 21:10).

AGAG. (1) Amalekite king mentioned in the prophecy of Balaam (Num. 24:7). (2) Amalekite king spared by Saul, killed by Samuel (I Sam. 15).

AGRIPPA I, HEROD. King of Judea (41–44 A.D.), a grandson of Herod the Great. He was a friend of the emperor Gaius Caligula, and was made king by his successor Claudius. Extravagant and heavily in debt before his change of fortune, he made a great show of Jewish piety as king. He ordered the execution of James, son of Zebedee, and the imprisonment of Peter (Acts 12). His public works included building a wall to protect Jerusalem on the north. He died suddenly of a disease at Caesarea.

AGRIPPA II, HEROD. By courtesy called king, but did not succeed his father Agrippa I. St. Paul was brought before him and his sister Berenice (Acts 25–26). He sought to stop the Jewish war with Rome, and ended his life in Italy.

AHAB. King of Israel, succeeded his father Omri and married Jezebel, daughter of Ithobaal, king of Tyre. Influenced by her, he allowed the worship of Baal to be promoted in Israel, but was opposed by the Prophet Elijah. In his rein there was war with the Syrians, yet near the close of his life he aided them against the Assyrians in association with Jehoshaphat king of Judah. He was killed at the Battle of Ramoth-Gilead (I Kings 20–22).

AHASUERUS. Probably the same as Xerxes, son of Darius I of Persia, reigned 485–465 B.C. Featured in the book of Esther and mentioned in Ezra 4:6 (See also **XERXES**).

AHAZ. King of Judah, who succeeded Jotham. He bought the help of Tiglath-Pileser III with part of the Temple treasure, to secure himself against the Syrians; accepting the overlordship of Assyria (II Kings 16). The Prophet Isaiah gave him a sign that Syria would cease to trouble him, but warned him against Assyria (Isa. 7).

AHIJAH. Prophet of Shiloh in the reign of Jeroboam I (I Kings 11:29).

AHIMELECH. Priest of Nob, who assisted David by giving consecrated loaves to him and his men. He was killed on the orders of Saul with the other priests of Nob, only his son Abiathar escaping (I Sam. 21–22).

AHITOPHEL. Counsellor in the reign of David who joined in the revolt of Absalom (II Sam. 15–16).

AKHENATEN (AMENOPHIS IV). Pharaoh of Egypt (c. 1370–1356 B.C.), who embraced the cult of Aten (the solar disc) in place of that of Amun-Re and the rest of the Egyptian pantheon with all their mythological trappings. He changed the capital of Egypt from Thebes to a new city, Akhetaten (Tell el-Amarna), where valuable letters have been found throwing light on relations with Palestine and other countries. His absorption in his faith cost Egypt her empire.

ALCIMUS. Hellenized Jewish priest made high priest (162–159 B.C.) by Demetrius I of Syria. He opposed the revolt of Judas Maccabaeus, and eventually died of a stroke. He became known as the wicked high priest (I Macc. 7, 9).

ALEXANDER THE GREAT. Macedonian king (356–323 B.C.). He succeeded his father Philip at the age of 20 and embarked on campaigns against Darius III which won for him the whole Persian empire. He was favorable to the Jews and offered sacrifices at Jerusalem. At Alexandria, which he founded, the Jews had special privileges. Alexander died tragically at Babylon at the height of his fame. (For some of his victories see Part IV, 400–300 B.C.).

ALEXANDER JANNAUS (103–76 B.C.). Jewish king of the Hasmonean dynasty, who extended his kingdom by military exploits. As high priest he was opposed by the Pharisees and he was ruthless in the treatment of the disaffected among his own people. He was succeeded by his widow Salome Alexandra, whom he advised to make peace with the Pharisees.

AMAZIAH. King of Judah whose history is recorded in II Kings 14.

AMOS. Prophet during the reign of Jeroboam II of Israel. He had been a shepherd at Tekoa in Judah, but was called to prophesy in Israel. His book is the oldest of the prophetic collections in the Bible.

AMRAM. Father of Miriam, Aaron and Moses by Jochebed in the last period of the sojourn of the Israelites in Egypt (Exod. 6:20).

ANANIAS (1) A disciple of Jesus who conspired with his wife Sapphira to retain part of the price of a property given to the Church (Acts 5). (2) A disciple in Damascus who restored Paul's sight (Acts 9). (3) A high priest under Herod of Chalcis, concerned in the prosecution of St. Paul (Acts 23, 24).

ANANUS. High priest under Agrippa II responsible for the death of James, brother of Jesus Christ (Jos. Antiq. XX. ix.). He was killed by the war party in the Jewish revolt against the Romans.

ANDREW. Apostle of Jesus and brother of St. Peter (John 1:40).

ANNAS (HANAN). High priest 6–15 A.D. Five of his sons and his son-in-law Joseph Caiaphas held the high priestly office. He was concerned in the interrogation of Jesus. (John 18).

ANTEDILUVIAN PATRIARCHS (see Gen. 4–5).

ANTIOCHUS IV (EPIPHANES). Seleucid king of Syria (175–164 B.C.), who attempted to convert the Jewish people to the Greek religion by force, and profaned the Temple by setting up an altar to Zeus Olympius. His intentions were thwarted by the Maccabaean rising (I Macc. 1–6; II Macc. 4–10).

ANTIPAS, HEROD. Son of Herod the Great and tetrarch of Galilee and Perea in the time of Jesus. The scandal of his marriage to his brother's wife Herodias, having divorced the daughter of the Arabian king Aretas, involved him with the Arabs and also led to the death of John the Baptist, whom Herod had imprisoned (Matt. 14). Jesus was brought before him at Jerusalem (Luke 23). His wife's ambitions and the complaints of his subjects caused his deposition and banishment to Gaul by the emperor Gaius Caligula.

ANTIPATER. Father of Herod the Great. He championed John Hyrcanus II against his ambitious brother Aristobulus. He was a friend of Julius Caesar and was made Roman governor of Judea (c. 55–43 B.C.).

ANTONY, MARK. After the death of Julius Caesar he controlled the East for the Romans and formed a liaison with Cleopatra of Egypt. He and Octavian, later the Emperor Augustus, made Herod, son of Antipater, king of Judea. Later he was in conflict with Octavian and was finally defeated at the Battle of Actium (31 B.C.). Antony and Cleopatra committed suicide in Egypt. Herod sided with the victor and was confirmed on the throne of Judea by Octavian.

APOLLONIUS OF TYANA. Greek sage of the 1st century A.D., born at Tyana in Cappadocia. He based his philosophy on the teaching of Pythagoras. Travelled widely to extend both his knowledge and experience, being regarded as a holy man and even as divine. He was credited with power to heal the sick and foretell the future, with knowledge of all languages and the innermost thoughts of men. At the end of his life he was arraigned before the emperor Domitian for sedition, released, and died in the reign of Nerva. A disciple, Damis of Nineveh, who accompanied him on his journeys recorded his life and teaching. Utilizing this and other sources, including letters of Apollonius, a definitive biography was compiled by Philostratus at the beginning of the 3rd century. Apollonius has been compared to Jesus, and his life throws much light on the production of the Gospels.

APOLLOS (APOLLONIUS). A learned Jew of Alexandria skilled in the interpretation of the Scriptures, who became a full disciple of Jesus at Ephesus (Acts 18). He was greatly esteemed by the church at Corinth (I Cor. 1), and was possibly the author of the Epistle to the Hebrews in the New Testament.

ARCHELAUS. Son of Herod the Great and designated to succeed him as king of the Jews. But the emperor Augustus first made him ethnarch of Judea, Samaria and Idumea (4 B.C.–6 A.D.). He was deposed for oppressive government and exiled to Vienne on the Rhône. He is mentioned in Matt. 2:22.

ARETAS (HARETATH). King of the Nabataeans (9 B.C.–40 A.D.). His daughter married Herod Antipas and was divorced in favor of Herodias. Aretas went to war with Herod and defeated him, but retired under Roman pressure. His governor at Damascus tried to capture St. Paul (II Cor. 11:32).

ARTAXERXES. Name of three kings of Persia. The one in the time of Ezra was probably Artaxerxes II (404–358 B.C.), while the one in the time of Nehemiah was more likely Artaxerxes I (465–432 B.C.).

ASHURBANIPAL. King of Assyria (668–627 B.C.), called in the Bible Asnapper (Ezra 4:10). He broke the power of Egypt, capturing Thebes. He was a patron of learning and a large part of his library at Nineveh has been recovered.

ATHALIAH. Daughter of Ahab and Jezebel, made herself queen of Judah on the death of Ahaziah, killing all his sons except the infant Jehoash who escaped (II Kings 11). She promoted Baal worship, but after six years was assassinated at the instigation of the high priest Jehoiada.

AUGUSTUS CAESAR (OCTAVIAN). Roman emperor (31 B.C.–14 A.D.). He was the adopted son of Julius Caesar, and after Caesar's assassination joined Mark Antony and Lepidus in a triumvirate which finally ended when Octavian defeated Mark Antony at the Battle of Actium. As the architect of the Roman Empire, Augustus organized the Provinces and systematized their payment of tribute (Luke 2:1). He was heralded by poets like Virgil as the creator of a Golden Age of peace and prosperity, and accepted from the East worship as a divine being and savior of humanity.

AZARIAH (UZZIAH). King of Judah in whose reign Isaiah began his prophetic career and the country suffered a great earthquake (Zech. 14:5). The king died a leper (II Kings 15).

BACCHIDES. Governor of the eastern province of the Seleucid Empire under Demetrius Soter. He was sent to pacify Judea and establish Alcimus as high priest. Later, after the Syrian forces commanded by Nicanor had been defeated by Judas Maccabaeus, he returned with a large army and overwhelmed the Jewish forces at the Battle of Elasa in which Judas was killed in 150 B.C. (I Macc. 7–9).

BALAAM. Midianite prophet. He was brought by the Moabites to curse Israel, but instead pronounced a blessing which included a famous passage concerning a star arising from Jacob, treated later as a messianic prophecy. He was killed in the Israelite attack on Midian (Num. 22–24, 31:8).

BAR-ABBAS. A Jewish leader imprisoned for participation in an armed rising against the Romans in the time of Pontius Pilate (Mark 15:7). When Jesus was arraigned before Pilate the governor offered the Jews the release of a prisoner at the Passover, either Bar-Abbas or Jesus. The crowd chose Bar-Abbas. Some sources give his name as Jesus Bar-Abbas.

BARAK. Called by the prophetess Deborah to defeat the forces of Sisera, general of the army of Jabin, the Canaanite king of Hazor (Judg. 4–5).

BAR-KOCHBA; SIMON. Leader of the second Jewish revolt against the Romans (132–135 A.D.). He was hailed as Messiah by Rabbi Akiba, the Son of a Star (Bar Kochba) of Num. 24:17. The Emperor Hadrian had to send for his ablest general Julius Severus to quell the revolt. Bar-Kochba was finally defeated and slain at Bettir. He was a ruthless leader, as has been confirmed by letters of his discovered in caves near the Dead Sea, and persecuted Jewish believers in Jesus for not joining him.

BARNABAS. Christian Levite from Cyprus, who befriended St. Paul and shared in his first missionary journey. His name was Joseph, and he was called Barnabas by the Christians on account of his generous spirit (Acts 4:36, 9:27, 12:25, 13–15).

BARTHOLOMEW. One of the Twelve Apostles. His first

name appears to have been Nathanael (John 1:45), Bar-Tholomew being the surname Son of Tolmai.

BARUCH. Scribe and loyal friend of the Prophet Jeremiah, for whom he acted as amanuensis (Jer. 22, 36). Several apocryphal books were written in his name.

BATHSHEBA. Wife of Uriah a Hittite whom David took, disposing of her husband by getting him killed in battle. Afterward David married her and she became the mother of Solomon (II Sam. 11–12).

BELSHAZZAR. Acted as Regent of Babylon for his father Nabonidus (553–545 B.C.). According to the book of Daniel, he was warned by Daniel of the coming overthrow of Babylon by the Medo-Persians (Dan. 5).

BENHADAD. Name of several kings of Syria (c. 890-790 B.C.) involved in war with the kings of Israel. Regarding Benhadad II see I Kings 20, II Kings 8 and Benhadad III see II Kings 13:24–25.

BENJAMIN. Youngest son of the patriarch Jacob by Rachel and brother of Joseph (Gen. 35, 42–45).

BERENICE. Daughter of Agrippa I, king of Judea. She married first Herod of Chalcis and after his death, Polemo king of Pontus. She was deeply attached to her brother Agrippa II and appeared with him at Caesarea when St. Paul was interrogated (Acts 25). She tried to mitigate Roman severity towards the Jews at the time of the Jewish revolt. Titus, son of the Roman emperor Vespasian, took her as his mistress, and but for Roman opposition would have married her and eventually made her Roman empress.

BEZALEEL. Craftsman responsible for much of the ornamental work of the Tabernacle in the Wilderness and its appointments (Exod. 35–38).

BOAZ. Farmer of Bethlehem who married the Moabitess Ruth and became the ancestor of David and of Jesus Christ (Bk. of Ruth).

CAIAPHAS, JOSEPH. High priest during the life of Christ, appointed to office by the governor Valerius Gratus. He was the son-in-law of the former high priest Annas and concerned in the conspiracy to destroy Jesus (John 11:49; Matt. 26:57). He was deposed by the legate of Syria, Vitellius, after the recall of Pontius Pilate in 36 A.D. (Jos. Antiq. XVIII. iv. 3).

CAIN. First son of Adam, who murdered his brother Abel (Gen. 4). A sign was set in his forehead, the brand of Cain, and he was banished to the land of Nod.

CALEB. One of the twelve representatives of Israel sent by Moses to spy out the Promised Land. He and Joshua were the only ones to advise invasion of Canaan (Num. 13–14).

CEPHAS (see **PETER**).

CLAUDIUS. Roman emperor 41–54 A.D. He installed Agrippa as king of Judea, and after his death had to deal with messianic agitation in Palestine and other parts of the Roman Empire. One of his measures to this end reported by Suetonius was to expel foreign Jews from Rome. The Christians Aquila and his wife Priscilla were affected by this edict (Acts 18:2). Much of St. Paul's missionary activities took place in this reign.

CLEMENT OF ROME. Traditionally bishop of Rome near the close of the first century A.D. Almost certainly author of an extant Letter to the Corinthians of great importance to early Church history. An early Homily (II Clement) is incorrectly attributed to him, and he figures in Judaeo-Christian works, the Clementine Homilies and Recognitions, Epistle to James, etc.

CLEOPATRA. Queen of Egypt 52–30 B.C. Through her relations with Mark Antony she obtained part of the coast of Palestine and the revenue of Jericho with its balsam, and schemed against Herod I. She had shared the throne with one brother, Ptolemy XIV, and after his death with his younger brother, Ptolemy XV, whom she caused to be killed, making her son by Julius Caesar co-regent. Her downfall came with the victory of Octavian at the Battle of Actium, and she committed suicide. Egypt was taken over as a Roman Province.

CYRENIUS (see **QUIRINIUS**).

CYRUS. King of Persia 551–538 B.C. His conquest of Babylon made him master of the East, and one of his first acts was to return the gods of the peoples in subjection to Babylon to their own countries. This policy enabled the exiled Jews to return to their land and begin rebuilding of the Temple at Jerusalem (Ezra 1–6 and see Isa. 44:28–45:1).

DANIEL. A prophetic figure among the Jews carried captive to Babylon by Nebuchadnezzar, whose story is related in the book bearing his name. Additions to this book magnifying the reputation of Daniel as a judge are included in the Apocrypha. The dreams and revelations of Daniel in the Bible belong to a much later period (c. 162 B.C.).

DARIUS I. King of Persia 522-486 B.C. known as Hystaspis. He consolidated the Persian Empire, creating 20 satrapies (provincial governments) and fixing their tribute. He introduced the gold coin called after him the daric. His confirmation of the rebuilding of the Temple is mentioned in Ezra 6.

DAVID. King of Israel c. 1010–970 B.C. Youngest son of Jesse, he tended sheep until his exploits against the Philistines made him a national hero. He also achieved fame as a poet and singer and many of his compositions are in the book of Psalms. Succeeding to the throne of Saul, who had persecuted him, he extended the territory of Israel and made Jerusalem the capital. The dramatic story of his life begins at I Sam. 16.

DEBORAH. Prophetess who inspired Barak to rescue Israel from the Canaanites (Judg. 4–5).

DEMETRIUS I (SOTER). Seleucid king of Syria 162-150 B.C. He made Alcimus Jewish high priest, and his commander Bacchides finally succeeded in overcoming Judas Maccabaeus (I Macc. 7–10).

DINAH. Daughter of Jacob and Leah (Gen. 30:21, 34).

DOMITIAN. Roman emperor 81–96 A.D. Son of Vespasian, he succeeded his brother Titus. He was a tyrannical ruler hostile to Jews and Christians. His autocratic character is reflected in his insistence on being addressed as "our Lord and our God," and he figures in the book of Revelation. The Gospels of Matthew and Luke were probably published in his reign. He was assassinated in 96 A.D.

EHUD. Judge who delivered Israel from Eglon, king of Moab (Judg. 3).

ELI. High priest of Israel at Shiloh. The Prophet Samuel as a child was placed in his care. He was disgraced by his two sons and died on learning that the Ark of the Covenant had been captured by the Philistines (I Sam. 2–4).

ELIJAH. Prophet of Israel of the 9th century B.C. It was his mission to challenge the growth of Baal worship in Israel fostered by Ahab's queen Jezebel. He was a typical representative of the dervish-like schools of the prophets, and became a legendary figure even in his lifetime. From the story that he had been taken up to heaven the belief arose that he would return in the Last Days before the coming of the Messiah to call Israel again to repentance. Jesus declared that John the Baptist was the embodiment of his spirit.

ELISHA. Disciple of Elijah, and his successor, who played a considerable part in political affairs.

ELIZABETH. Wife of the priest Zachariah and mother of John the Baptist. According to Luke's Gospel she was related to Mary, the mother of Jesus (Luke 1:36).

ENOCH. Antediluvian patriarch noted for his piety. From the curious reference to his death (Gen. 5:24) it was inferred that he was translated to heaven (Heb. 11:5). The apocryphal books of Enoch dealt with his heavenly experience (quoted by Jude 14–15) and visions of the Last Days.

ESARHADDON. King of Assyria 680-668 B.C. Son of Sennacherib, who was murdered by two of Esarhaddon's brothers (II Kings 19:37). He subdued Egypt and in his reign Assyria reached the zenith of its power.

ESAU. Firstborn twin brother of the patriarch Jacob, defrauded of his birthright (Gen. 25). He became a desert chieftain centered on Mt. Seir.

ESTHER. Also called by the Hebrew name Hadassah (myrtle). Heroine of the historical romance which bears her name. As queen of the Persian king Ahasuerus she saves her people from the jealous revenge of Haman. The book explains the origin of the Jewish feast of Purim.

EVIL-MERODACH. King of Babylon 561-560 B.C. Succeeded Nebuchadnezzar II. He released Jehoiachin, former king of Judah, from prison (II Kings 25:27).

EZEKIEL. Jewish priest and third of the Major Prophets of the Bible. He was among the captives carried to Babylon by Nebuchadnezzar, and saw his earlier visions by the Euphrates canal called Chebar. The latter part of his book describes the future restoration of Israel and the Temple in ideal terms.

EZRA. Scribe of priestly descent who led one of the contingents of Jewish exiles in the return from Babylon. He devoted himself zealously to eliminating from Jewish life and worship all taint of heathenism (books of Ezra-Nehemiah), and is credited with laying the foundations of the canon of the Old Testament. The date of his activities is uncertain, but probably in the reign of Artaxerxes II (404-358 B.C.).

FADUS, CUSPIUS. Roman governor of Judea appointed by Claudius on the death of Agrippa I (44 A.D.). He ruthlessly suppressed patriotic and messianic outbreaks, including, it would appear, proceedings against the Judaeo-Christians.

FELIX, ANTONIUS. Roman governor of Judea 52-59 A.D. Took as his second wife Drusilla third daughter of Agrippa I. He was noted for his cruelty and rapacity during his term of office, and was recalled by Nero, escaping punishment only through the influence of his brother Pallas. He kept St. Paul imprisoned at Caesarea because no bribe was forthcoming (Acts 23–24).

FESTUS, PORCIUS. Roman governor of Judea 60-62 A.D. One of the better procurators. St. Paul refused his proposal to be tried by the hostile Sadducean Council at Jerusalem and appealed to Caesar (Acts 25). Festus died not long after and was succeeded by Albinus.

FLORUS, GESSIUS. Roman governor of Judea 64–66 A.D. His folly and greed finally forced the Jews into open revolt against the Romans.

GAIUS CALIGULA. Roman emperor 37–41 A.D. A vain and eccentric ruler readily persuaded that he was really divine. His attempt to have his statue as Jupiter set up in the Temple at Jerusalem nearly caused a Jewish revolt. The situation was saved only by the moderation of Petronius, Roman legate of Syria, and the assassination of the emperor. The circumstances are reflected in Matt. 24:15; II Thess. 2:4.

GALLIO, LUCIUS. Brother of the Stoic philosopher Seneca, and Roman proconsul of Achaia (51-52 A.D.), when St. Paul was accused before him at Corinth (Acts 18:12–17).

GAMALIEL I. Grandson of Hillel and a leading member of the Great Sanhedrin, noted for his moderation. St. Paul had been a pupil of his (Acts 22:3), and he advised against extreme action against Peter and John (Acts 5:34–39).

GEDALIAH. Made Jewish governor of Judea by Nebuchadnezzar, but assassinated after two months (II Kings 25; Jer. 41). The day of his death is kept as a Jewish fast.

GIDEON. Also called Jerubaal, one of the notable judges of Israel who defeated the Midianites. His story is told in Judg. 6–8.

GOLIATH. Giant champion of the Philistines slain by David (I Sam. 17).

GORGIAS. Syrian general in the service of Antiochus Epiphanes charged with destroying the forces of the Maccabees (I Macc. 3–5).

HABAKKUK. One of the Minor Prophets of the Bible. His brief book reflects the Chaldean invasion of Judah early in the 6th century B.C.

HAGAR. Egyptian servant of Sarah, wife of the patriarch Abraham, given to him to provide him with offspring. She became the mother of Ishmael. Later when Sarah herself had a son Isaac, her jealousy compelled Abraham to send away Hagar and Ishmael (Gen. 16, 21).

HAGGAI. One of the Minor Prophets after the return from Babylon. In conjunction with Zechariah he encouraged the people under Zerubbabel to rebuild the Temple.

HAMMURABI. Sixth Amorite king of the first dynasty of Babylon (c. 1724-1682 B.C.). He was the architect of the first Babylonian Empire, covering nearly all Mesopotamia, and was famed for his Code of Laws. His identification with Amraphel king of Shinar (Gen. 14:1) is regarded as very doubtful.

HAZAEL. King of Syria, exceptionally anointed by a Hebrew prophet, Elisha, (I Kings 19:15; II Kings 8:7–15). He succeeded Benhadad II, whom he murdered. While he oppressed Israel, he strongly resisted the Assyrians under Shalmaneser II (c. 841 B.C.).

HEGESIPPUS. Early Church historian of Jewish origin who wrote in the second half of the 2nd century A.D. His

Memoirs in five books are lost, but extracts preserved by Eusebius in his Ecclesiastical History are an important source of information on the sub-apostolic period.

HEROD I. Called the Great, king of Judea 37–4 B.C. He obtained the throne by virtue of his friendship with Mark Antony and Octavian, and maintained his position by skilled diplomacy and ruthlessness towards opponents. A Jew by religion, he was detested by his people for his alien (Idumean) origin, his devotion to the Romans and to heathen Hellenic culture. Continually in fear of plots and conspiracies, he put to death many of his relations and friends. His lavish rebuilding of the Temple at Jerusalem failed to appease Jewish hostility and his death was widely welcomed. At the close of his reign Jesus Christ was born, and according to Matthew 2 was very nearly the victim of the tyrant's jealous rage.

HERODIAS. Her illegal second marriage to Herod Antipas was one of the causes of the death of John the Baptist who had denounced the union (Matt. 14). She was the mother of Salome.

HEZEKIAH. King of Judah. Noted for his endeavors to uphold the worship of Yahweh and suppress idolatry, counselled by the Prophet Isaiah. When he began to reign the kingdom of Israel had fallen before the Assyrians (722 B.C.), but he was able to prevent their attempt to overthrow Judah (II Kings 18–20; Isa. 36–39).

HILKIAH. High priest in the reign of Josiah, king of Judah. He discovered the book of the Law in the Temple, a circumstance which contributed to the king's reforming policy.

HILLEL. Famed Jewish spiritual leader of the Herodian period. He came to Jerusalem from Babylon to study religious doctrine and was reputed to be descended from David. A pious and moderate man, he rose between 30 B.C. and 10 A.D. to be elder of the Sanhedrin and leader of the Pharisees, a teacher whose wisdom and saintliness was widely revered. He had numerous disciples, who created a school of thought known as Bet Hillel (the House of Hillel), and many of his sayings have been preserved, some of which seem to have been known by Jesus.

HIRAM. Particularly the king of Tyre who was in league

with David and Solomon, and furnished timber and craftsmen for the building of the Temple at Jerusalem (I Kings 5–7).

HOSEA. A prophet of the 8th century B.C. in the reign of Jeroboam II king of Israel. In his prophetic message he used the adultery of his own wife to illustrate the apostasy of Israel in language of great pathos and spiritual understanding.

HYRCANUS I, JOHN. High priest and king of the Jews 134–104 B.C. He was the son of Simon Maccabaeus, and in his reign succeeded in restoring complete independence to the Jewish people and in extending their territory. He was regarded by many as a figure of messianic significance, combining the offices of prophet, priest, and king.

HYRCANUS II, JOHN. Ill-fated elder son of King Alexander Jannaeus, who served as high priest 78–40 B.C. Opposed by his ambitious younger brother Aristobulus, he was used as a pawn in a game of power politics which brought his country under Roman domination. After many vicissitudes and changes of fortune he was put to death by Herod in 30 B.C.

ISAAC. Second of the Hebrew patriarchs, son of Abraham and Sarah in their old age. As a child he submitted to the prospect of being offered up as a sacrifice by his father, a test of Abraham's trust in God (Gen. 22). His life was semi-nomadic. By Rebekah, a kinswoman, he had twin sons Esau and Jacob.

ISAIAH. First of the Major Prophets of the Bible, lived in the 8th century B.C. in the reign of Uzziah, Jotham, Ahaz and Hezekiah, kings of Judah. He was a man of great vision, ability and political influence, and his prophetic works have been an abiding source of inspiration. The messages of a later unknown prophet of the 6th century have been added to his writings, and are often described as Second Isaiah.

ISHBOSHETH. The name has been substituted for Ishbaal, Son of Saul, first king of Israel. The attempt was made by Saul's general Abner to seat him on the throne after his father's death in battle. But regarding himself as insulted by Ishbosheth, Abner went over to David. Ishbosheth was murdered not long after, to David's great distress (II Sam. 2–4).

ISHMAEL. Son of Abraham by Hagar. He became a nomad chieftain.

ISRAEL (see **JACOB**).

ITHAMAR. Youngest son of Aaron, the first high priest of Israel. He superintended the assembly of materials for the Tabernacle (Exod. 38:21). His descendants held the high priesthood from Eli to Abiathar.

JABIN. Canaanite king of Hazor, and head of a powerful confederacy defeated by Joshua. He was killed in the capture of Hazor (Josh. 11).

JACOB. Third of the Hebrew patriarchs and son of Isaac. The story of his life commences in Gen. 25. He received the name of **ISRAEL** (Gen. 32) and was the father of twelve sons by his wives Leah and Rachel, and their handmaidens Bilhah and Zilpah, who gave rise to the twelve tribes of Israel. His favorite was Joseph, sold by his brothers into slavery, but who became vizier of Egypt. In old age Jacob settled in Egypt and died there, but his body was embalmed and taken to Canaan and buried in the family tomb of the cave of Machpelah.

JAEL. A Kenite woman, who entertained and killed Sisera, the defeated general of Jabin II, king of Hazor, after the battle with the Israelite forces under Barak (Judg. 4).

JAMES (JACOB). Brother of Jesus, who became head of the Christian community (Gal. 1:19; Acts 15). Early tradition described him as a devout Jew and a pious ascetic highly regarded by the Jewish people. He was executed by the Sadducean Council on a trumped-up charge in 62 A.D. and was buried at Jerusalem. Josephus records that the Pharisees protested about this action to the new governor Albinus (Antiq. XX, ix, 1). **(2) SON OF ZEBEDEE** (see **JOHN**).

JEHOASH (JOASH). King of Judah c. 835–796 B.C. In his reign of forty years he repaired the Temple at Jerusalem, but later used the wealth of the Sanctuary to buy off Hazael, king of Assyria. He died by assassination (II Kings 12).

JEHOASH (2). King of Israel c. 798–783 B.C. He was present at the death of the Prophet Elisha. He contended successfully with the Syrians, and also fought and defeated Amaziah, king of Judah, carrying off the treasures of the Temple to Samaria (II Kings 13–14).

JEHOIACHIN. King of Judah 598–597 B.C. After a brief reign he was sent to Babylon by Nebuchadnezzar, accepting with his family honorable captivity. Babylonian records confirm that he was well treated (II Kings 24–25).

JEHOIADA. High priest in the reign of Jehoash, king of Judah. He acted as regent during the king's minority and assisted him in his reforms. He died at an advanced age (II Chron. 23–24).

JEHOIAKIM. King of Judah 609–598 B.C. Placed on the throne by Pharaoh Necho, he became subject to Babylon. He was a reckless ruler who favored heathen rites and listened to unwise counsellors, persecuting the prophets of Yahweh. Rebelling against Nebuchadnezzar, he was crushed by the Babylonian forces (II Kings 23–24; Jer. 26, 36).

JEHOSHAPHAT. King of Judah c. 870–848 B.C. A successful ruler who put down heathenism, but allied himself with Ahab, king of Israel, and nearly lost his life at the Battle of Ramoth-Gilead (II Chron. 17–20; I Kings 22).

JEHU. King of Israel c. 841–814 B.C. General of the forces of King Ahab, he was anointed by the Prophet Elisha and seized the throne by a coup, exterminating his opponents. He secured his government by becoming tributary to the Assyrians under Shalmaneser III, recorded on the black obelisk of that monarch, (II Kings 9–10).

JEPHTHAH. Judge of Israel who delivered them from the Ammonites. His daughter became the victim of his rash vow (Judg. 11–12).

JEREMIAH. Second of the Major Prophets. It was his destiny to prophesy in the last days of the kingdom of Judah, when his counsel was rejected, to accept the inevitability of Babylonian domination. He suffered persecution and imprisonment and finally took refuge in Egypt. His denunciations and uncompromising demand for national repentance made him detested in court circles, but he had the ear of the people. He foresaw the return from the Babylonian exile.

JEROBOAM I. First king of the separate kingdom of Israel. The prophet Ahijah told him he would be given the rule of ten tribes out of the kingdom of Solomon. When Solomon sought to kill him he fled to Egypt, returning when the king was dead and bringing about the secession from Solomon's son Rehoboam. To keep the people from joining with Judah in worshipping at the Temple at Jerusalem he reconsecrated sanctuaries at Dan and Bethel with worship of a golden calf. (I Kings 11–13).

JEROBOAM II. King of Israel c. 783–743 B.C. He is denounced for encouraging idolatry like Jeroboam I, but extended his territory by military successes (II Kings 14 and book of Amos).

JESUS (JASON). Ill-famed high priest of the 2nd century B.C., who adopted the Greek way of life and changed his name to Jason. He obtained his office from Antiochus Epiphanes by bribery, but after three years was deposed and died in exile (II Macc. 4–5).

JESUS BEN SIRA. A Jewish scholar who lived near the beginning of the 2nd century B.C. in Jerusalem. His fame rests on his moral teaching in a book translated into Greek by his grandson. The work is included in the Biblical Apocrypha under the name Ecclesiasticus. The major part of the Hebrew text has been recovered.

JOAB. A nephew of David, king of Israel, and for many years commander of his forces. He was a successful soldier, but personally ambitious and vindictive. His treacherous killing of his opponent Abner and later of David's rebellious son Absalom exhibited a ruthlessness which became intolerable. Involved in the plot to secure the throne of David's son Adonijah, his execution was ordered by Solomon, the son David had chosen to succeed him (II Sam. 2–3, 18–19; I Kings 1–2).

JOHANAN BEN ZAKKAI. Eminent Jewish scholar of the 1st century A.D. He foretold the destruction of the Temple, and was convinced that the Romans would defeat the Jews because the rebels cared little for the divine laws. He had himself conveyed out of the besieged city of Jerusalem in a coffin and after the war established the seat of religious authority at Jabneh (Jamnia). It was his spiritual leadership which helped to overcome Jewish despair and gave an impetus to the development of Judaism.

JOHN THE BAPTIST. A prophetic figure of priestly descent at the beginning of the Christian era. From the wilderness of Judea he proclaimed the near advent of the Kingdom of God, calling upon the people to repent and be dipped in the Jordan. Some believed him to be the Messiah and the chief reason he was imprisoned and later executed by order of Herod Antipas seems to have been that his proclamation would lead to an uprising. The Gospels present him as the forerunner of the Messiah, acknowledging him in Jesus when he came to be baptized. Luke makes him a kinsman of Jesus. The cause of John's death is given in the Gospels as due to the jealousy of Herodias whose illegal marriage to Herod Antipas the Baptist had denounced. A sect arose which held John to be the Messiah.

JOHN OF GISCALA. A Galilean who became one of the Jewish leaders in the war with Rome. He had been the opponent of Josephus, who held the Jewish command in Galilee, and later in Jerusalem was involved in the power struggle for control of the city. He fought ably against the Romans, and did not surrender until the whole of Jerusalem was in their hands. Carried to Rome for the triumph of Titus he is believed to have died in captivity.

JOHN AND JAMES, SONS OF ZEBEDEE. Brothers included in the Twelve Apostles, who received from Jesus the nickname of Boanerges (the tempestuous). With Peter, they were closest to Jesus, and the same three were the pillars of the early Church. James was executed by Agrippa I, and it is traditional that John also perished. The identification of John with the Beloved Disciple of the Fourth Gospel and with the seer of the Revelation is very doubtful. This was probably another John who died at an advanced age at Ephesus.

JONATHAN. Son of Saul, king of Israel, and close friend of David, whom he saved from his father's jealous rage. His exploits against the Philistines and his personal charm endeared him to the people. His death in the Battle of Mt. Gilboa was movingly lamented by David (II Sam. 1). His history is related in I Sam. 14–20, 23, 31.

JONATHAN MACCABAEUS. Assisted his brother Judas in the Jewish revolt against Antiochus Epiphanes. When Judas fell in battle Jonathan was chosen to succeed him as leader. From 160–143 B.C. he fought the Syrians and used his diplomatic skill in the rivalries for the throne of the Seleucids to win for the Jews a position of relative independence. He also officiated as high priest. He was killed by Trypho, who headed one of the Syrian factions, and was succeeded by his brother Simon (I Macc. 9–13).

JOSEPH. Son of the patriarch Jacob by Rachel. He was sold into slavery by his brothers and brought to Egypt where, after vicissitudes, he rose to high rank as chief officer of Pharaoh. He was able to help his brothers in a time of great famine and finally settled them and their families in Egypt in the land of Goshen. He married the daughter of the Egyptian priest of On, and had sons Ephraim and Manasseh. His dreams and the capacity to interpret dreams play an important part in his history, and he came to be regarded as the ideal perfect man. (Gen. 37:1).

JOSEPH (2). Husband of Mary, mother of Jesus. He appears only in the accounts of the birth and childhood of Jesus in the Gospels of Matthew and Luke, but mentioned otherwise as a carpenter and father of a large family. **(3) JOSEPH OF ARIMATHEA,** a wealthy Jewish counselor and secret disciple of Jesus. He obtained the body of Jesus from Pilate and buried him in his own tomb.

JOSEPHUS, FLAVIUS. Jewish historian of priestly stock. He was born Joseph ben Matthias in 37 or 38 A.D. and took his Roman name from the Flavian family of his patron, the Emperor Vespasian. At the outbreak of the Jewish revolt he was appointed commander in Galilee, and surrendered to the Romans at the fall of Jotapata. He claims to have told Vespasian that he would be emperor, and obtained his protection and subsequent friendship. After the war he accompanied Vespasian's son Titus to Rome and received Roman citizenship and honors. He died early in the reign of Trajan, having devoted his later years to an account of the **Jewish War,** the **Antiquities of the Jews,** an apologetic work **Against Apion,** etc., which allowing for his circumstances and prejudices are of great historical importance.

JOSHUA. Able commander under Moses during the wandering of the Israelites in the wilderness. Moses gave him the charge of leading the Israelites in the conquest of Canaan after the Lawgiver's death. The Biblical book named from him relates how he fulfilled his mission. The events may be dated in the second half of the 13th century B.C.

JOSIAH. King of Judah c. 637–609 B.C. He was called to the throne at the age of eight after the murder of his father Amon, and as a young man became noted for his zeal in putting down heathen worship following the discovery of the Book of the Law in the Temple. He died in battle fighting the forces of Pharaoh Necho at Megiddo (II Kings 22–23).

JUDAH. Fourth son of Jacob by Leah. He came to take a leading position among the sons of Jacob (Gen. 44:14) and the tribe descended from him eventually became dominant and gave rise to the Jewish people (Judeans) and Jewish faith (Judaism). Prophetically, the civil government was vested in Judah as the spiritual was vested in Levi.

JUDAS OF GALILEE. Leader of a resistance movement to Roman domination of Palestine, proclaiming that God alone was Ruler of the Jews. He was born at Gamala in Gaulonitis, and in 6 A.D. opposed the Roman census for taxation instituted by the Emperor Augustus (Luke 2:1; Acts 5:37). He was probably killed fighting the Romans, but the movement he founded, sometimes called the Galileans, continued the struggle led by his sons Jacob and Simon, who were crucified under Fadus and Alexander in the reign of Claudius. Another son, or perhaps grandson, Menahem, claimed the messiahship in the revolt of 66 A.D.

JUDAS ISCARIOT. One of the Twelve Apostles. The surname may mean that he came from the town of Kerioth in Judah or that he had belonged to the resistance movement afterwards known as Sicarii (dagger men). According to John's Gospel (12:6) he acted as purser to the band of disciples. He betrayed Jesus to the authorities, and in remorse committed suicide (Matt. 26–27).

JUDAS MACCABAEUS. One of the sons of Mattathias the priest who with his brothers organized revolt against the attempt of Antiochus Epiphanes to impose the Greek faith on the Jews. He waged successful guerilla warfare and raised an army that could meet and defeat the Syrian troops. In 165 B.C. he restored Jewish worship in the Temple, commemorated in the festival of Dedication (Chanukah). His heroic career ended in 160 B.C. when he fell in battle against greatly superior forces (I Macc.).

KORAH. Levitical leader who with Dathan and Abriam opposed the authority of Moses and Aaron. Their death by an earthquake is described as an act of God in Num. 16.

PART VIII

NOTABLE NAMES (L-Z)

LABAN. Kinsman of Abraham who lived in Aram-nahariam (Mesopotamia). His sister married Isaac, and two of his daughters married Isaac's son Jacob. His nature is revealed as selfish and avaricious. (Gen. 24–25, 28–31).

LEAH. Elder daughter of Laban, whom he married to Jacob by a subterfuge (Gen. 29:3). She bore Jacob six sons and a daughter Dinah. On her death she was buried in the Cave of Machpelah.

LEVI. Third son of Jacob by Leah. He was the ancestor of Moses, and the tribe of Levi was chosen as the priestly tribe of Israel.

LEVI-MATTHEW (see **MATTHEW**).

LOT. Nephew of Abraham, who traveled with him to Canaan after the death of his father. Later he separated from Abraham and settled in the region of the Dead Sea, where he was captured by an invading army attacking the cities of the plain, but rescued by the retainers of Abraham. Warned by angels, Lot and his family fled from Sodom before its overthrow. The ancestry of the peoples of Moab and Ammon is attributed to the incestuous relations of the daughters of Lot with their father (Gen. 19).

LUKE. Christian physician and companion of Paul (Col. 4:14; II Tim. 4:11). To him is attributed the Gospel of Luke and the Acts of the Apostles.

MANASSEH. Succeeded Hezekiah as king of Judah and reigned for fifty-five years. He encouraged the return of idolatrous practices. The sins of Manasseh are held up as an awful warning (II Kings 21). He was taken captive by the Assyrians to Babylon, but according to II Chron. 33 he repented in captivity and was restored to his throne. The Prayer of Manasseh is included in the books of the Apocrypha.

MARIAMNE. Tragic Hasmonean princess married to Herod the Great. While Herod loved her greatly, his fears of plots against him led him to listen to accusations by his sister that Mariamne had been guilty of adultery and subsequently had sought to poison him. In the end she was executed after being imprisoned, but Herod was deeply affected and embittered by her death.

MARK, JOHN. Son of Mary, the sister of Barnabas. He accompanied Paul and Barnabas on their joint missionary journey, but soon returned to Jerusalem. On the next journey Barnabas wished to take Mark with them again, but Paul refused, and they separated. There was an eventual reconciliation between Mark and Paul (Col. 4:10; II Tim. 4:11). Mark assisted Peter (I Pet. 5:13), and tradition makes him Peter's interpeter and author of Mark's Gospel based on notes of Peter's addresses. He is held to have evangelized Egypt and to have died at Alexandria, but there is no reliable evidence about this.

MARY MAGDALENE. A devoted follower of Jesus, who had cured her of a grave disorder (possession by seven demons, Mark 16:9; Luke 8:2). There is no evidence that she had ever been a prostitute. She assisted Jesus with her means, was present at the crucifixion, and was one of the women who came to pay his body their last respects and found the tomb empty. John records how the risen Jesus revealed himself to her (John 20). The name Magdalene indicates that she came from Magdala in Galilee.

MATTATHIAS OF MODIN. Aged Jewish priest who refused to make an idolatrous sacrifice as required by an officer of Antiochus Epiphanes, and killed the officer and a Jew who was willing to sacrifice. Escaping with his sons, he initiated the revolt of which his son Judas Maccabaeus was the leader (I Macc. 2).

MATTHEW. Also called Levi. One of the Twelve Apostles. Until his call by Jesus he had been a tax collector and Jewish outcast (Matt. 9:9). He became the author of certain records about Jesus written in Hebrew no longer extant; some of this material in a Greek translation may have been a source used in the Gospel attributed to Matthew.

MENAHEM. King of Israel in the middle of the 8th century B.C. He seized the throne by killing his predecessor Shallum, who in turn had killed the previous monarch. He paid tribute to Tiglath-Pileser, king of Assyria, to gain security and protection, making a levy of 50 shekels of silver on all the wealthy men of Israel (II Kings 15:14–21).

MEPHIBOSHETH. Corruption of Mephibaal. Son of Jonathan and thus grandson of Saul, first king of Israel. He was made a cripple when his nurse fled with him and let him fall (II Sam. 4:4). David, who had been Jonathan's friend, restored to him Saul's estate; but Mephibosheth was later implicated in Absalom's revolt, though he appears to have been the tool of Saul's former servant Ziba (II Sam. 16:3, 19:24–30).

MERNEPTAH. Pharaoh of Egypt c. 1234–1225 B.C. Son of the famous Rameses II, and with strong probability ruler of Egypt at the time of the Exodus of the Israelites. He had to meet attacks from the west by Libyans allied with the Peoples of the Sea, and earlier he appears to have sent an expedition to Palestine. Victory hymns of his reign include a claim to have defeated Israel.

MERODACH-BALADAN (Marduk-apal-iddina III). Babylonian king near the close of the 8th century B.C. who was a sturdy opponent of Assyria. Seeking to strengthen himself in the struggle, he sent an embassy to Hezekiah, king of Judah (II Kings 20:13). The Assyrians were still powerful, however, and Merodach-Baladan was several times defeated. His reign, none the less, heralded the end of Assyrian tyranny.

METHUSELAH. One of the antediluvian patriarchs credited with living 969 years.

MICAH. One of the Minor Prophets, and a younger contemporary of Isaiah. He came from Moresheth-Gath near the Mediterranean coast. In his prophecies he attacked the moral and social evils of his time and looked forward to an era of righteousness. His reference to a ruler who should come from

Bethlehem (Mic. 5:2) was later interpreted as a prediction of the Messiah.

MICHAL. Daughter of Saul, king of Israel, given in marriage to David (I Sam. 18:17–28). She aided his escape from her father's jealous vengeance; but Saul then gave her to Phalti, son of Laish (I Sam. 25:44).

MORDECAI. Cousin of Esther, and hero of the book of Esther. He saves the life of King Ahasuerus by disclosing a plot to murder him, and Mordecai's foe Haman, who seeks to destroy the Jews, is forced to pay him honor. With Haman's downfall and execution on the gallows he had intended for Mordecai, the hero is raised to the highest dignity and the Jews are saved from the destruction planned by Haman.

MOSES. The greatest name in the history and religious development of Israel. Brought up as an Egyptian prince, he became the leader and deliverer of Israel from servitude to the Egyptians. At Sinai he received from God the Ten Commandments and the divine laws, endured much opposition and rebelliousness of his people, and finally brought them to the frontiers of the Promised Land. His nobility and generosity of spirit continually appears in the records contained in the five books of the Bible (Genesis to Deuteronomy) named after him as the books of Moses.

NAAMAN. Commander of the forces of the king of Syria. Elisha the prophet was instrumental in curing of his leprosy. He became converted to the God of Israel. The story in II Kings 5 is a little masterpiece.

NABONIDUS. King of Babylon c. 556–539 B.C. Last ruler of the Neo-Babylonian Empire, which wilted rapidly with Medo-Persian expansion. He was more interested in archaeology than politics, and his son Belshazzar largely acted for him.

NABOPOLASSAR. King of Babylon c. 625–605 B.C. Chaldean ruler who created the Neo-Babylonian Empire after effectively contributing to the destruction of Assyria with the help of Medes and Scythians.

NADAB AND ABIHU. Sons of Aaron, destroyed for offering "strange fire" before the Lord (Lev. 10:1–7).

NAHUM. One of the Minor Prophets. In graphic language he spoke of the fall of Nineveh (Nah. 3).

NATHAN. Prophet in the reigns of David and Solomon in close contact with the court. The book of his prophecies and experiences is lost, together with the works of other prophets of the period (I Chron. 29:29; II Chron. 9:29). He denounced David for taking Bathsheba and causing the death of her husband (II Sam. 12).

NATHANIEL. One of the first who accepted Jesus as Messiah (John 1:45–50). He may be the same as Bar-Tholomew, one of the Twelve Apostles.

NEBUCHADNEZZAR. Greatest ruler of the Neo-Babylonian Empire (c. 605–562 B.C.), son of Nabopolassar. He was a truly imperial figure in his various military exploits, his statesmanship, and the magnificence with which he surrounded himself in the city of Babylon, which he reconstructed and adorned. In the Bible he appears as the destroyer of the Temple and the kingdom of Judah; and the book of Daniel tells of the humbling of his pride and his acknowledgment of Israel's God.

NECHO II. Pharaoh of Egypt c. 609–594 B.C. He intervened in the struggle between Babylon and Assyria, probably with some aim to control Palestine and Syria. He defeated and killed Josiah, king of Judah, at Megiddo (II Kings 23:29) and pushed on to the Euphrates, where he was held and returned to Egypt, but still keeping Judah under his thumb. Later the forces of Necho again confronted the Babylonians at Carchemish on the Euphrates. This time the Egyptians were decisively defeated by Nebuchadnezzar (see above), who at the time was crown prince of Babylon.

NEHEMIAH. A pious and patriotic Jew who held office as cup-bearer to the Persian king Artaxerxes I at Susa. He obtained authority to visit Jerusalem and repair the walls of the city in 445 B.C. He was successful in his mission despite opposition from peoples hostile to the Jews, the work was completed, and the services in the Temple were fully restored. Nehemiah, called also the Tirshatha (Governor), is traditionally credited with founding a library in which were collected the surviving Hebrew archives from which sprang the Bible. He paid a second visit to Jerusalem in 433, when he dealt with various abuses which had grown up in his absence.

NERO. Roman emperor 54–68 A.D. He was a despotic ruler; vain, cruel, and profligate. At the time of the Great Fire in Rome in 54 A.D. he singled out the Christians as the alleged incendiaries and had them tortured and destroyed. It is believed that both St. Paul and St. Peter suffered under him. When the Jewish revolt broke out in Judea Nero sent Vespasian to quell it; but while the war raged he was forced from his throne and ignominiously committed suicide. Legend had it that Nero had not died, but escaped to the east and would return to wreak vengeance on the Rome which had turned against him.

NICANOR. Seleucid general. Later, under Demetrius I, made governor of Judea. He is described in the books of Maccabees as the enemy of the Jews. Having failed to seize Judas Maccabaeus by treachery, Nicanor led the Syrian army against him, but was defeated and killed. The Jewish victory in 161 B.C. was long after observed as a festival known as Nicanor's Day, observed on the 13th of the month Adar (I Macc. 7; II Macc. 14–15).

NICODEMUS. Member of the Jewish Council friendly to Jesus. He appears only in the Fourth Gospel. He sought an interview with Jesus by night (John 3) and later tried to protect him (John 7:50–52) and after the death of Jesus brought spices for his burial (John 19:39).

NICOLAS OF DAMASCUS. Friend and confidant of Herod the Great, to whose history Josephus was largely indebted for information on this king's reign. Nicolas acted for Herod on several important missions.

NOAH. The hero of the Biblical story of the Flood. He and his family were saved by building an Ark at God's command and bringing into it pairs of every kind of animal. When the waters abated the Ark rested on the mountains of Ararat. From the sons of Noah, Shem, Ham and Japheth, the nations were divided (Gen. 5–10).

OMRI. King of Israel c. 885–874 B.C. He was commander of the forces of Israel and made king because of the treachery of Zimri, who had seized the throne by murdering the former king Baasha and destroying his family. With Omri a new dynasty was created, known in the Assyrian records as the "house of Omri." He changed the capital of Israel from Tirzah to Samaria (I Kings 16).

ONIAS III. Jewish high priest at the beginning of the 2nd century B.C. He opposed the Hellenizing influences which were corrupting the purity of Judaism, but was ousted from office and finally had to escape to Daphne, near Antioch, where he was assassinated. He became a legendary figure (II Macc. 3–4).

ONIAS IV. Probably the son of Onias III. He sought the protection of Egypt when he failed to secure the high priesthood, and was permitted by Ptolemy VI to build a Jewish temple at Leontopolis.

OTHNIEL. Younger brother of Caleb, he was the first of the Judges of Israel (Judg. 1:12, 3:8).

PAPIAS. Bishop of Hierapolis in Phrygia about the second quarter of the 2nd century A.D. His importance is due to his preservation of oral traditions of the life and teaching of Jesus, obtained from those who had seen and heard some of the apostles, and to statements made by him about the origin of the Gospels. Using the information he had collected, he composed a work of five books entitled **Exposition of the Oracles pertaining to the Lord,** of which only a few fragments have survived in quotation.

PAUL. Christian Apostle to the Gentiles, first known by his Hebrew name Saul. Born at Tarsus in Cilicia, of a Jewish family possessing Roman citizenship, and educated at Jerusalem under the Pharisee authority Gamaliel I. He was a young man at the time of the Crucifixion and was violently antagonistic to the Nazarene movement. As a result of a vision on the road to Damascus he changed suddenly from persecutor to disciple, and became the foremost exponent of Christianity to non-Jews, traveling widely in Asia Minor and Greece and founding a network of churches. The Acts of the Apostles is largely devoted to his career and a substantial part of the New Testament is occupied by his epistles. We know more of Paul than of any of the Apostles, and he was the first to work out a systematic Christian philosophy in which he employed a knowledge of mystical Judaism which he related to the needs of those familiar with the soteriology of the mystery cults. He may be said to have created Christianity as a distinct religion. His life ended in Rome c. 6 A.D. where he was brought as a prisoner after he had appealed to Caesar; but the circumstances of his condemnation and execution are uncertain.

PETER, SIMON. The most outstanding of the immediate followers of Jesus and chief of the Apostolic band. A humble fisherman of Galilee, he was called with his brother Andrew, and nicknamed Cepha (Greek **Petros,** rock) because of his solid devotion. It became his function to lead and strengthen the disciples when they were deprived of the presence of Jesus. Through his instrumentality the door of faith was opened to Gentiles with the conversion of the centurion Cornelius. Handing over the government of the Church to James, the brother of Jesus, he is believed to have spent the remainder of his life as an itinerant evangelist with special concern for the Jewish people, and to have suffered martyrdom at Rome during the Neronian persecution. Two epistles in his name are included in the New Testament, but the authenticity of the second is regarded as most doubtful.

PHILIP. One of the Twelve Apostles, more particularly mentioned in the Fourth Gospel.

PHILIP THE DEACON. One of seven Greek-speaking Christians appointed to deal with the material needs of the Church at Jerusalem (Acts 6). An account of his missionary work is given in Acts 8. He took up residence at Caesaria and had four unmarried daughters (Acts 21:8–9).

PHILIP THE TETRARCH. Son of Herod the Great, who inherited the northeastern provinces of his kingdom. It was he who converted Panias at the source of the Jordan into the city of Caesarea-Philippi (Matt. 16:13), in honor of Augustus, and also changed the name of Bethsaida at the northeast of the Lake of Galilee to Julias, in honor of the emperor's daughter. Near this Bethsaida the feeding of the 5000 took place (Luke 9:10–17). Philip married his niece Salome, daughter of Herodias, who as a girl had asked for the head of John the Baptist (Matt. 16:4–11). He died in 34 A.D.

PHILO OF ALEXANDRIA. Sometimes called Philo Judaeus (c. 20 B.C.–50 A.D.). A famous Hellenistic-Jewish philosopher belonging to an influential Alexandrian family, he made his aim in life to present the teaching of the Bible in terms which would appeal to the educated Greek, employing freely the art of allegory developed by the Stoics. His personification of the Divine Wisdom (Logos) proved useful to nascent Christianity, and is echoed in the Epistle to the Hebrews, but his method had little effect on contemporary Judaism. Philo much admired the Essenes and their Egyptian counterparts the Therapeutae. When advanced in years he went on an embassy to Rome to attempt to persuade the Emperor not to force the Jews to worship his image, a design in which the emperor had been encouraged by anti-Jewish elements in Alexandria. Most of Philo's numerous writings are extant, largely due to preservation by the Christian Church, which greatly admired him.

PHINEHAS. Son of Eleazar and grandson of Aaron. As a result of his action recorded in Num. 25 he received the covenant of a perpetual priesthood. In late messianic thought, Phinehas was held to have been taken to heaven and became identified with Elijah as the precursor of the final redemption of Israel.

PILATE, PONTIUS. Roman governor of Judea and Samaria 25–36 A.D. His term of office was from the beginning marked by great intolerance in his attitude towards the religious scruples of the Jews and Samaritans. He seemed determined to assert the authority of Rome and override all opposition as may be seen in the incidents recorded by Josephus. If, as indicated in the Gospels, he was reluctant to order the execution of Jesus, it was probably because he wished to humiliate the Jewish Council. Hence his insistence when forced to give way, on crucifying Jesus as "King of the Jews." Because of his arrogance and ruthlessness he was recalled by the emperor Tiberius, who died however before Pilate reached Rome.

PLATO. Athenian philosopher born in 427 B.C. His teaching regarding an ideal world society and the immortality of the soul did much to prepare Hellenic thought for the reception of Christianity. Through the **Dialogues** he conveyed not only the mind of Socrates, but his own conceptions, which emerge particularly in the **Republic,** the **Georgics,** the **Timaeus** and the **Phaedrus.**

PLINY THE YOUNGER. Roman advocate c. 61–115 A.D. He was a nephew of Pliny the Naturalist, who lost his life at the eruption of Vesuvius in 79 A.D. He held increasingly high office and early in the 2nd century was governor of Bithynia under Trajan. His letter to Trajan in which he reports on the treatment of Christians and seeks approval of his course of action is of great interest and importance.

POMPEY (CN. POMPEIUS). With Julius Caesar and Crassus he was a member of the first Roman triumvirate. His importance for Biblical history rests on his activities in Palestine, where in 63 B.C. he was called upon to settle the rival claims of the Hasmonean princes, the brothers John Hyrcanus II and Aristobulus II. The folly of Aristobulus and his supporters compelled Pompey to besiege and capture Jerusalem, where he committed the grave offense of entering the holy place of the Temple. This earned him the execration of pious Jews as expressed in the **Psalms of Solomon,** and it was felt that he had met a just fate, when after his defeat by Caesar he was murdered by his former supporters on landing in Egypt.

QUIRINIUS, P. SULPICIUS. Roman legate of Syria who instituted the census of the Jews decreed by Augustus Caesar as mentioned in Luke 2:1–3. This was carried out in 6–7 A.D. after the deposition of Archelaus as ethnarch, and was bitterly resented, causing some under Judas of Galilee to resist in arms.

RACHEL. Favorite wife of the patriarch Jacob, who served her father Laban altogether fourteen years. By her Jacob had two sons, Joseph and Benjamin. Rachel died in giving birth to Benjamin, and was buried on the road to Bethlehem (Gen. 35:16–20).

REBEKAH. Wife of the patriarch Isaac. She was the sister of Laban, and the romantic story of how she became Isaac's wife is told in Gen. 24. She was the mother of twin sons, Esau and Jacob, and persuaded Jacob to obtain by a trick the blessing of the firstborn properly belonging to Esau (Gen. 27).

REHOBOAM. Son of Solomon and his successor as king of Israel. Yielding to the representations of his young courtiers he gave a harsh reply to the people who petitioned him for relief from the oppressive laws imposed by Solomon. This action lost him the greater part of his kingdom, thus fulfilling a prophecy, and he reigned only over Judah and Benjamin at Jerusalem (I Kings 12). In the fifth year of his reign the Egyptian king Sheshonq invaded Judah and plundered the Temple.

RUTH. The Moabitess who is the heroine of the book of

Ruth, and who by her marriage to Boaz became the ancestor of King David.

SAMSON. One of the Judges of Israel who helped Israel against the Philistines, he was noted for his great strength. From the angelic promise of his birth to his heroic death the life of Samson is told in terms of Herculean exploits (Judg. 13–16).

SAMUEL. Last of the Judges and revered Prophet. From infancy he was dedicated to the service of God, and in manhood ruled Israel with justice. Reluctantly he gave way to the people's demand for a king, and anointed first Saul, and when he proved unsuitable, chose David in his stead. When he died and was buried at Ramah all Israel mourned his passing. The story of his life is told in the first book of Samuel.

SANBALLAT. Called the Horonite. He was the leading opponent of Nehemiah and tried to prevent the Jews from rebuilding the walls of Jerusalem. His influence was evidently very powerful and a daughter of his was married to a son of the high priest Eliashib. He is several times referred to in the book of Nehemiah and also in Josephus' **Antiquities,** XI. vii. 2.

SARGON II. King of Assyria (c. 821–705 B.C.). He was one of the most powerful of the kings of Assyria and reigned in Babylon also. In his achievements he somewhat resembled his namesake Sargon I of Agade, who had lived fifteen hundred years earlier and of whose infancy a story was told resembling that of Moses. Sargon completed the destruction of the kingdom of Israel begun by his predecessor Shalmaneser, capturing Samaria in 722 and deporting many of its inhabitants. All Palestine paid him tribute after the siege and capture of Ashdod (Isa. 20:1). He was killed in a military expedition to the far north and succeeded by his son Sennacherib.

SAUL. Son of Kish, first king of Israel (c. 1030–1010 B.C.). In presence, stature, and physical courage, Saul fitted the popular conception of a king, as demanded by Israel in their petition to Samuel. But he was psychologically unstable and developed paranoid tendencies. He was deeply dependent on Samuel, and when the aged prophet abandoned him and anointed David as his successor, the effect on Saul was disastrous. He brooded on his wrongs and attempted to destroy David. But there was much goodness in him inherited by his son and heir Jonathan. Both died tragically in battle against the Philistines. Saul's story is told in I Sam. 8–31.

SAUL OF TARSUS (See **PAUL**).

SELEUCUS NICATOR. One of the generals of Alexander the Great, who inherited the eastern provinces of the short-lived Macedonian Empire, (312–280 B.C.) and founded the Seleucid dynasty.

SENECA. Roman philosopher of the Stoic school (c. 1-65 A.D.) and brother of Gallio, proconsul of Achaia, mentioned in the Acts of the Apostles. He was entrusted with the education of the young Nero, who came to detest his moralizing but refused to allow him to retire from public life. Finally, on a charge of being implicated in Piso's conspiracy, he was ordered by Nero to commit suicide. Some of Seneca's teaching is similar to that of St. Paul; but he disliked the Jews and criticized their tenets and customs.

SENNACHERIB. King of Assyria (705–681 B.C.), son and successor to Sargon II. He was faced with the task of restoring the suzerainty of Assyria over the western peoples, who had stopped paying tribute when Sargon was killed. In a series of campaigns he succeeded, but when he overran Judah, ruled by Hezekiah, he failed to capture Jerusalem. His arrogant threats find a place in the book of Kings (II Kings 18) and in the prophecies of Isaiah (8-10). A mysterious plague attacked the Assyrian forces, killing a host of them. Sennacherib was forced to return to Nineveh, where he was murdered in the temple by his sons Adrammelech and Sharezer (II Kings 19:37).

SIMEON SON OF CLEOPHAS. Succeeded his cousin James, the brother of Jesus, as head of the Christian community. He was elected to office by the apostles and relations of Jesus surviving in 70 A.D. at the end of the Jewish war with the Romans. Early tradition has it that he lived until the reign of the Emperor Trajan, when he was denounced to the Romans as a descendant of David and a Christian, and suffered martyrdom.

SIMON BAR-GIORA. Jewish leader in the revolt against Rome. He was born, it is believed, at Gerasa. He was a militant patriot and guilty of ruthless action in maintaining the struggle, and until the Romans seriously threatened Jerusalem, engaged in constant strife with the rival Jewish forces under John of Giscala. The opposing groups then united, and Simon proved a bold and inspiring general. Captured by the Romans he was brought to Rome for the triumph of Titus and executed.

SIMON THE JUST. High priest. It is not certain whether he is to be identified with the successor of Onias I or Onias II, probably the latter. In any case he will have lived in the third century B.C. He is lauded and his activities are described by Jesus ben Sira in the Apocrypha (Ecclus. 1). His reputation for piety caused him to be made a figure of legend, and he exemplified theocratic government at its best.

SIMON THE MACCABEE. One of the gallant brothers, sons of the priest Mattathias, who fought for the Jewish faith against the Syrians. He became leader of the Jewish people with the capture and death of his brother Jonathan, and was confirmed as high priest, military commander and ethnarch in perpetuity. His generalship and political sagacity achieved real independence for the Jews, whom he ruled from 143 to his murder in 135 by a son-in-law. With Simon the Hasmonean dynasty was founded (I Macc. 13–16).

SIMON MAGUS. A Samaritan who made extravagant spiritual claims for himself, and became a Christian to serve his own ends (Acts 8:9–34). Little for certain is known about him; but legend built him up as a magician and sorcerer, head of a Gnostic sect, and the determined opponent of the true faith as represented by Simon Peter (Clementine **Homilies** and **Recognitions**). Some have seen in the Ebionite portrayal of him a caricature of the Apostle Paul.

SIMON PETER (see **PETER**).

SISERA. Defeated general of the forces of Jabin, king of Hazor, in the deliverance wrought by the Judge of Israel Barak, inspired by the prophetess Deborah. Fleeing from the battle Sisera was treacherously killed by a Kenite woman Jael, with whom he had accepted refuge (Judg. 4–5).

SOLOMON. King of Israel (970–931 B.C.), son of David by Bathsheba. To assure his succession David placed him on the throne in his own lifetime. Solomon became famed for his wisdom and magnificence. He consolidated his position by alliance with the surrounding sovereigns and contracting marriages with daughters of the royal houses. Internally, he organized the political and economic life of the country, and sponsored commercial enterprises and foreign trade, so that he speedily achieved unprecedented power and prosperity. He was a great lover of horses, and maintained large cavalry and chariot forces. His reputation for knowledge and grandeur traveled far and wide, leading to the famed visit of the Queen of Sheba. He put into effect his father's plan to build a Temple for God at Jerusalem, lavishing upon the edifice all the wealth and resources at his command, so that it was a wonder of workmanship and design. With similar magnificence he built his own palace "the house of the forest of Lebanon" (I Kings 10:16–21). The Biblical accounts of Solomon's reign describe his glory in legendary terms. In the times of the golden king, silver counted for nothing (I Kings 10:21). His wisdom exceeded that of all the children of the east, and all the wisdom of Egypt . . . He uttered three thousand proverbs, and composed one thousand and five songs (I Kings 4:29–34). Yet in the end his greatness proved his undoing, and yielding to his foreign wives he sponsored the worship of alien gods. On this account adversaries were raised against him (I Kings 11). Some of the biblical psalms and proverbs may be among the literary remains of Solomon, and he is alluded to in the Song of Songs. As a messianic type, several extra-canonical works employ his name.

STEPHEN. Known as the first Christian martyr. He was one of the seven Hellenist Jewish believers to be made a deacon, and was brought before the Sanhedrin on a charge of blasphemy. His defence (Acts 7) so aroused antagonistic feeling that he was rushed out of Jerusalem and stoned to death, one of the approving onlookers being Saul of Tarsus.

THEUDAS. A Jewish false prophet who attempted to lead the Jews in an anti-Roman rising when Cuspius Fadus was governor of Judea (c. 45 A.D.). Fadus sent a force against him, and his head was brought to Jerusalem (Josephus **Antiq.** XX. v. 1). The Acts (5:36) mistakenly places the activity of Theudas before that of Judas of Galilee, probably because Josephus had mentioned the execution of the two sons of Judas immediately after his reference to Theudas.

THUTMOSE III. The most powerful of the Egyptian Pharaohs (c. 1500–1450 B.C.). In fifteen campaigns he made himself master of Palestine and Syria and much of Western

Asia. With the spoils he gathered he carried out vast building operations, including the hall of columns of the Temple of Amun-Re at Karnak.

TIBERIUS CAESAR. Roman emperor 14–37 A.D. The reign of this emperor covered the period of the ministry and crucifixion of Jesus, and his character to an extent contributed to what happened at Jerusalem in the governorship of Pontius Pilate. The elderly emperor, living in retirement at Capri, was much under the influence of Sejanus, who to advance his own ambitions did his utmost to make Tiberius distrustful of all who stood in his way. As a result, a reign of terror spread through the Roman empire with many innocent persons denounced and arrested for treason. Spies and informers abounded. Finally realizing what was happening Tiberius took action against Sejanus and had him executed. One of the emperor's last actions was to recall Pontius Pilate from Judea.

TIGLATH-PILESER III. One of the most powerful of the kings of Assyria (c. 745–727 B.C.). In the Bible he is called Pul, in II Kings 15:19, but his full name is given in the following chapter. He had to contend with Syrian attempts to revolt against Assyrian suzerainty. Menahem, king of Israel, paid a heavy bribe to maintain his throne, and Ahaz, king of Judah, sought Tiglath-Pileser's aid to secure himself against the Assyrians. The Assyrians responded, besieged Damascus and put an end to the power of Syria in 732. Israel, which had sided with the Syrians, was shorn of much of its territory, and Hoshea was made puppet king of what was left (II Kings 15–16; Isa. 7–8).

TIMOTHY (TIMOTHEUS). Son of a Greek father and Jewish mother, whom Paul took as his assistant on his second visit to Lystra, and who became his devoted companion and helper. Timothy's name is joined with that of Paul in a number of Paul's epistles, and he was sent to various churches to sustain and encourage them in their faith. Timothy was with Paul on his last journey to Jerusalem, and Paul sent for him to be with him at the time of his last trial at Rome. Paul's letters to Timothy show the affection which existed between them, and how grateful the apostle was to have such a son in faith.

TITUS. Roman emperor 79–81 A.D. in succession to his father Vespasian. When Vespasian was proclaimed emperor in Palestine he left Titus in command to complete the suppression of the Jewish revolt, which he accomplished successfully with the destruction of Jerusalem after a prolonged siege in 70 A.D. It was said that he tried to spare the Temple, but his troops could not be restrained. He was the friend of Agrippa II and enamored of his sister Berenice. Titus was accorded a triumph when he returned to Rome with the spoils of Jerusalem, commemorated by the Arch of Titus, which still stands.

TITUS (2). Companion of Paul, identified with the evangelization of Crete (Epistle to Titus).

TRAJAN. Roman emperor 98–117 A.D. A military man, he became a fairly tolerant ruler, mitigating some of the severity of the persecution of the Christians, if we are to rely on his letter to Pliny. But he had to contend with the revival of Jewish revolutionary activities in various parts of the empire and a cousin of Jesus, Simeon, son of Cleophas, was executed as a descendant of David and a Christian. Tacitus, the Roman historian, completed his **Histories** down to the end of Trajan's reign, and the same writer's **Annals** contains an early external reference to the death of Jesus (XV. lxiv).

UZZIAH (see **AZZARIAH**).

VESPASIAN. Roman emperor 70–79 A.D. As a veteran general he was called from retirement by Nero to put down the Jewish revolt in Palestine, and carried out his mission with grim relentlessness and in a systematic manner. Josephus, the Jewish commander in Galilee, surrendered to him and claimed to have prophesied that he would become emperor in fulfillment of Jewish messianic predictions. After Nero's death, and the swift passing of Galba, Otho and Vitellius, Vespasian was acclaimed by the legions and hastened to Italy, leaving his son Titus to finish the war in Judea.

VIRGIL (P. VERGILIUS MARO). Roman poet (c. 70-19 B.C.). The fourth of his Eclogues was of great interest to Christians since it predicted, on the basis of the Sibyl of Cumae, the birth of a boy in whose time the Golden Age would return.

XERXES (see **AHASUERUS**).

ZACHARIAS. Father of John the Baptist. He was a priest of the family of Abijah (I Chron. 24:10), married to Elizabeth, who was also of a priestly family, and according to Luke a kinswoman of Mary, the mother of Jesus. He and his wife received a divine promise of a son in their old age, who should be dedicated to God and the forerunner of the Messiah. Early tradition declares that when Herod killed the babes in Bethlehem in order to destroy the infant Messiah, the mother of John fled with him into the wilderness, and Zacharias was slain because he would not reveal the whereabouts of his son. There is evidence that the Gospel story and other traditions depend on a Nativity Story of John the Baptist in which he was hailed as the Messiah, circulated by the followers of the Baptist.

ZADOK. Priest of the line of Eleazar, son of Aaron, in the reigns of David and Solomon. His loyalty to David and his successor was rewarded with the high priesthood. Zadok in fact anointed Solomon as king over Israel. The Zadokite line of high priests continued until the time of the Maccabees.

ZECHARIAH. One of the twelve Minor Prophets who with Haggai encouraged the Jewish people to rebuild Jerusalem and the Temple after the return from the Babylonian exile. The prophecies of Zechariah are notable for their apocalyptic visions.

ZEDEKIAH. Last king of Judah (c. 598–587 B.C.). He was made king by Nebuchadnezzar, who changed his name from Mattaniah to Zedekiah (II Kings 24:17–18). Neglecting the warnings of the Prophet Jeremiah (Jer. 37–39), he rebelled against Nebuchadnezzar, who besieged and captured Jerusalem. Zedekiah, endeavoring to escape, was captured by the Chaldeans. His sons were killed before his eyes, and then he was blinded and taken in chains to Babylon where he died.

ZERUBBABEL. Son of Shealtiel and of the royal line of David. He led the first return of Jewish captives from Babylon under the decree of Cyrus permitting the restoration of the Temple at Jerusalem. With him was the high priest Jeshua (Ezra 2–6). Much opposition was encountered from the people of the land, which greatly delayed the rebuilding of the Temple; but Zerubbabel seems to have survived to see the completion in the reign of Darius I. He held office as governor of Judah on behalf of the Persians. Further references to him are to be found in the books of Haggai and Zechariah.

PART IX

TABLES AND GENEALOGIES

High Priests from Aaron to the Babylonian Exile—High Priests in the Time of the Second Temple—The Kings of Israel and Judah—The Ptolemaic Dynasty of Egypt—The Seleucid Dynasty of Syria—The Hasmonean Dynasty of Judea—The Herodian Family in Relation to the New Testament—Roman Governors of Judea to 70 A.D.

In ancient times great care was taken to maintain and preserve genealogical records, particularly of families in the regal and priestly lines. To be able to trace back one's ancestry not only conferred a certain status; it was also important in connection with property. The Bible contains a great many lists and tables, which may often be boring to read, but which in many cases cannot be neglected as sources of information and historical knowledge. In their time, especially after the return from the Babylonian Exile, such records were of vital consequence. There is no need to repeat here the records which the Bible provides in its genealogical passages. But there are tables which are not exactly set out, such as those of the high priests and of the kings of Israel and Judah. When we come to the intertestamental period and the New Testament other lists which are given in this Part are essential to enable the reader to follow intelligently the sequence of events and the position and relationship of prominent individuals.

HIGH PRIESTS FROM AARON TO THE BABYLONIAN EXILE

The principal sources are the Bible and the **Antiquities** of Josephus. These do not exactly tally, but a late Jewish list in the **Seder 'Olam Zuta** favors Josephus and helps to complete the table. Names not in the Bible are given in italics.

AARON
ELEAZAR
(Line of Eleazar)
PHINEHAS
ABISHUA
BUKKI
UZZI (I Chron. 6:3–5)
(Line of Ithamar son of Aaron)
ELI (I Sam. 1:3)
AHITUB (I Chron. 9:11)
AHIAR (I Sam. 14:3)
AHIMELECH (I Sam. 21:1)
ABIATHAR (I Sam. 33:6)
(Line of Eleazar Resumed)
ZADOK (I Kings 2:35)
AHIMAAZ (II Sam. 15:36)
AZARIAH I (I Kings 4:2)
Joram or *Joash*
JEHOIARIB (I Chron. 9:10)
Jehoshaphat
JEHOIADA (II Kings 11:4)
Pedaiah
Zedekiah
AZARIAH II (II Chron. 26:17) or *Joel*
Jotham
URIJAH (II Kings 16:10)
AZARIAH III (II Chron. 31:10) or *Neriah*
Hoshaiah
SHALLUM (I Chron. 6:12)
HILKIAH (II Kings 22:4)
AZARIAH IV (I Chron. 6:13)
SERAIAH (II Kings 25:18)
JEHOZADAK (I Chron. 6:14)

HIGH PRIESTS IN THE TIME OF THE SECOND TEMPLE

The last high priest to be mentioned in the Old Testament is Jaddua, but the line from Zadok continued to hold office until the high priesthood was taken over by the Hasmoneans after the Maccabaean Revolt. The Hasmonean line continued until the time of Herod, and from then on the high priests were appointed at the will of the rulers, both Jewish and Roman, mainly from powerful and rich priestly families. These high priests were frequently deposed from office and ceased to serve for life or for as long as they were ritually fit as formerly. Deputy high priests were also appointed. The New Testament speaks in the plural of "chief priests" because ex-high priests and ex-deputies were often living at the same time and serving as members of the Jewish Council over which the reigning high priest presided. One of the high priests mentioned in the New Testament Annas (Hanan) had no less than five sons and a son-in-law (Joseph Caiaphas) who at various times held the office of high priest. The sources for the list are the Old Testament, Apocrypha and Josephus.

JESHUA (Hag. 1:1)
JOIAKIM (Neh. 12:10)
ELIASHIB (Neh. 3:1)
JOIADA (Neh. 12:10)
JOHANAN (Neh. 12:22)
JADDUA (Neh. 12:22)
ONIAS I
SIMON I
ELEAZAR
MANASSEH
ONIAS II
SIMON II (Ecclus. 1)
ONIAS III (I Macc. 12:7)
JESUS (Jason), (II Macc. 4:7)
MENELAUS (II Macc. 4:27)
ALCIMUS (I Macc. 7:5)
(Hasmonean High Priests)
JONATHAN son of Mattathias (I Macc. 9:28)

SIMON son of Mattathias (I Macc. 14:46)
JOHN HYRCANUS I son of Simon (I Macc. 16:23)
ARISTOBULUS I
ALEXANDER JANNAEUS
JOHN HYRCANUS II
ARISTOBULUS II
JOHN HYRCANUS (resumed office)
ANTIGONUS
(Appointed by Herod the Great)
HANANEEL (not a Hasmonean)
ARISTOBULUS III (last Hasmonean High Priest)
HANANEEL (resumed office)
JESUS son of Phabet
SIMON son of Boethus
MATTATHIAS son of Theophilus
JOSEPH son of Ellem (deputized once for **MATTATHIAS**)
JOAZAR son of Boethus
(Appointed by Archelaus)
ELEAZAR son of Boethus
JESUS son of Sie
JOAZZAR son of Boethus (reappointed)
(Appointed by Quirinius)
ANNAS (Hanan) son of Seth (Luke 3:2)
(Appointed by Valerius Gratus)
ISHMAEL son of Phabi
ELEAZAR son of Annas
SIMON son of Kamith
JOSEPH CAIAPHAS son-in-law of Annas (Matt. 26:3)
(Appointed by Vitellius)
JONATHAN son of Annas (perhaps the John of Acts 4:6)
THEOPHILUS son of Annas
(Appointed by Agrippa I)
SIMON KANTHERAS son of Boethus
MATTATHIAS son of Annas
ELIONEUS son of Kantheras
(Appointed by Herod of Chalcis)
JOSEPH son of Kamus or Kamydus (perhaps Kamith)
ANANIAS son of Nebedeus (Acts 23:2)
JONATHAN son of Annas (reappointed)
(Appointed by Agrippa II)
ISHMAEL son of Phabi (reappointed)
JOSEPH CABI son of Simon (Kantheras ?)
ANANUS (**Annas**) son of Annas (executed James the brother of Jesus)
JESUS son of Damneus
JESUS son of Gamaliel
MATTATHIAS son of Theophilus
(Appointed by the People in the War with Rome)
PHINEHAS son of Samuel

With reappointments this brings the total of high priests

from Aaron to Phinehas to eighty-three, the number given by Josephus (**Antiq.** XX. x). Appointments to the office ceased with the destruction of the Temple in 70 A.D.

THE KINGS OF ISRAEL AND JUDAH

The sources of our knowledge of the kings of Israel and Judah are the First and Second Book of Kings and the Second Book of Chronicles, works which derive their information chiefly from the lost Annals of the reigns of the different kings. The only chronology furnished by the Bible is the lengths of the various reigns together with indications of how far the kings of Israel and Judah were contemporary until the extinction of the kingdom of Israel. The chronology is assisted, however, by numerous references to the rulers of other countries, Egypt, Syria, Assyria and Babylon. Recovered records from these countries, including the Assyrian Eponym List and the Babylonian Chronicle, now help to date the reigns of the Hebrew Monarchy often with a considerable degree of certainty. It is still best, however, to treat all figures given as approximate. Prior to the division of the kingdom **DAVID** had reigned 40 years (1010-970) I Kings 2:11, and his son **SOLOMON** had also reigned 40 years (970-931) I Kings 11:42.

	ISRAEL		JUDAH
(931–910)	JEROBOAM I (I Kings 14:20)	(931–913)	REHOBOAM (I Kings 14:21)
(910–909)	NADAB (I Kings 15:25)	(913–911)	ABIJAM (I Kings 15:1–2)
(909–886)	BAASHA (I Kings 15:33)	(911–870)	ASA (I Kings 15:9–10)
(886–885)	ELAH (I Kings 16:8)		
(885)	ZIMRI (I Kings 16:15)		
(885–874)	OMRI (I Kings 16:23)		

Assyria: ASHURNASIRPAL II (884–859)

(874–853) AHAB (I Kings 16:29)
(853–852) AHAZIAH (I Kings 22:51)

(870–848) JEHOSHAPHAT (I Kings 22:41–42)

Assyria: SHALMANESER III (859–824)

(852–841) JEHORAM (II Kings 3:1)
(841–814) JEHU (II Kings 10:36)
(814–798) JEHOAHAZ (II Kings 13:1)
(798–783) JEHOASH (II Kings 13:10)

(848–841) JEHORAM (II Kings 8:16–17)
(841) AHAZIAH (II Kings 8:25)
(841–835) ATHALIAH (II Kings 11:3)
(835–796) JEHOASH (II Kings 12:1)
(796–781) AMAZIAH (II Kings 14:2)

Assyria: ADAD-NIRARI III (810–782)

(783–743) JEROBOAM II (II Kings 14:23)
(743) ZECHARIAH (II Kings 15:8)
(743) SHALLUM (II Kings 15:13)
(743–738) MENAHEM (II Kings 15:17)

(781–740) AZARIAH (II Kings 15:2)
(740–736) JOTHAM (II Kings 15:32)

Assyria: TIGLATH-PILESER III (745–727)

(738–736) PEKAHIAH (II Kings 15:23)
(737–732) PEKAH (II Kings 15:27)
(732–724) HOSHEA (II Kings 17:1)

(736–716) AHAZ (II Kings 16:2)
(716–687) HEZEKIAH (II Kings 18:2)

Assyria: SHALMANESER V (727–722)
SARGON II (722–705)
SENNACHERIB (705–681)

The Kingdom of Israel came to an end in 722 B.C. and from this date we are dealing only with the Kingdom of Judah. But the whole of the 8th century B.C. presents serious chronological problems, as the biblical data relating to the kings of this period, the length of their reigns and the correspondences between the respective rulers of each kingdom, cannot be fitted into what scholars regard as a probable scheme in the light of external information.

Judah only

(687–642) **MANASSEH** (II Kings 21:1)

Assyria: **ESARHADDON** (681–669)
ASHURBANIPAL (669–661)

(642–640) **AMON** (II Kings 21:19)
(640–609) **JOSIAH** (II Kings 22:1)

Babylon: **NABOPOLASSAR** (625–605)

(609) **JEHOAHAZ** (II Kings 23:31)
(609–598) **JEHOIAKIM** (II Kings 23:36)
(598) **JEHOIACHIN** (II Kings 24:8)
(598–587) **ZEDEKIAH** (II Kings 24:18)

Babylon: **NEBUCHADNEZZAR** (605–562)

THE PTOLEMAIC DYNASTY OF EGYPT

The dynasty of the Ptolemies in Egypt and that of the Seleucids in Syria, described in Daniel 11 as the King of the South and the King of the North, chiefly affected the fortunes of the Jewish people from the time of Alexander the Great to the rise of the Maccabees or Hasmoneans, but continued to be of consequence until the Romans became masters of the Near East (see Part IV, **DOWN THE CENTURIES**). The founder of the Ptolemaic dynasty was Ptolemy Lagus, but the Ptolemies are numbered from his son, who assumed the title of king in 305 B.C.

PTOLEMY I (Soter) 305–285 (abdicated)
PTOLEMY II (Philadelphus) 285–247
PTOLEMY III (Euergetes) 247–222
PTOLEMY IV (Philopator) 222–205
PTOLEMY V (Epiphanes) 205–181
PTOLEMY VI (Eupator) 181
PTOLEMY VII (Philometor) 181–146
(reigned jointly with his brother Euergetes
(afterwards Ptolemy IX) 170–165)
PTOLEMY VIII (Philopator Neos) 146
PTOLEMY IX or **EUERGETES II** (Physcon) 146–117
PTOLEMY X or **SOTER II** (Lathyrus) 117–81

(reigned jointly with his mother Cleopatra 117–107, banished and restored in 87)
PTOLEMY XI or **ALEXANDER I,** 107–89
(co-regent with his mother Cleopatra)
PTOLEMY XII or **ALEXANDER II,** 81
PTOLEMY XIII (Auletes) 81–52
PTOLEMY XIV, 52–47
(reigned jointly with his sister the famous Cleopatra)
PTOLEMY XV, 47–45
(younger brother of Ptolemy XV, was co-regent with Cleopatra, who had him killed and replaced by her son by Julius Caesar, Caesarion.
PTOLEMY XVI or **CAESARION**
(co-regent with Cleopatra)

THE SELEUCID DYNASTY OF SYRIA

SELEUCUS I (Nicator) 312–280
ANTIOCHUS I (Soter) 280–261
ANTIOCHUS II (Theos) 261–246
SELEUCUS II (Callinicus) 246–226
SELEUCUS III (Ceraunus) 226–223
ANTIOCHUS III, THE GREAT 223–187
SELEUCUS IV (Philopator) 187–175
ANTIOCHUS IV (Epiphanes) 175–164
ANTIOCHUS V (Eupator) 164–162
DEMETRIUS I (Soter) 162–150
Alexander Balas, a usurper, 150–146
DEMETRIUS II (Nicator) 146–138
(taken prisoner by the Parthians)
Antiochus VI (Theos) son of Alexander Balas, 144–142
Diodotus Tryphon, 142–137
ANTIOCHUS VII (Sidetes) 137–128
DEMETRIUS II, reigned again 128–125

From this time there were sometimes two or three rival rulers.

Alexander Zabinas, 127–122
ANTIOCHUS VIII (Gryphus) 125–96
SELEUCUS V (Nicator) 125–123
ANTIOCHUS IX (Cyzicenus) 111–95

SELEUCUS VI (Epiphanes) 95–94
ANTIOCHUS X (Eusebes) 95–83
ANTIOCHUS XI (Epiphanes II) 94–83
DEMETRIUS III (Eucaerus) 94–83
Tigranes, The Great, 83–69
ANTIOCHUS XII (Dionysius) 69–65
ANTIOCHUS XIII (Asiaticus) 69–65

THE HASMONEAN DYNASTY OF JUDEA

The creation of the Hasmonean dynasty was the outcome of the successful revolt against the attempt of the Seleucid king Antiochus Epiphanes to impose Hellenic worship on the Jews. The revolt was organized by the priest Mattathias of the Hasmonean family and his five sons John, Simon, Judas called Maccabaeus, Eleazar, and Jonathan. As a result the Jews gradually regained their independence. Judas was killed in battle, and Jonathan was then appointed as Jewish leader. When he was murdered he was succeeded by Simon, with whom the dynasty began. The Hasmoneans are also known as the Maccabees from the nickname of Judas. They held the high priesthood as well as the civil authority.

SIMON (142–135)
(Assassinated with two of his sons Judas and Mattathias and succeeded by his third son John Hyrcanus)
JOHN HYRCANUS I (135–104)
ARISTOBULUS I (104–103)
(Succeeded by his brother Alexander who married Salome Alexandra the widow of Aristobulus)
ALEXANDER JANNAEUS (103–76)
ALEXANDRA (76–67)
(Her eldest son John Hyrcanus was high priest, but her younger son Aristobulus seized the civil power on her death)
ARISTOBULUS II (67–63)
(He was deposed by Pompey and his brother John was made Jewish ethnarch as well as high priest)

JOHN HYRCANUS II (63–40)
(John was captured by the Parthians and his nephew Antigonus son of Aristobulus became king)
ANTIGONUS (40–37)
(Herod the Great was made king by the Romans and had Antigonus executed. Herod married the Hasmonean princess Mariamne a granddaughter of John Hyrcanus.)

THE HERODIAN FAMILY IN RELATION TO THE NEW TESTAMENT

Herod the Great had ten wives, by eight of whom he had nine sons and five daughters. The table given here traces the descendants of four wives only, since these were more directly concerned with Jewish history and include all members of the Herodian family mentioned in the New Testament. Names not of interest in either connection are omitted. There was a good deal of intermarriage in the family and the following cases are to be noted especially: (1) Herod the Great's son Aristobulus by Mariamne the Hasmonean married Berenice daughter of Salome, Herod's sister; (2) Herodias was married first to Herod's son Herod-Philip and second to his half-brother Herod Antipas; (3) Salome, daughter of Herodias and Herod-Philip, married her uncle Philip the Tetrarch; (4) Berenice, daughter of Agrippa I, married second her uncle Herod of Chalcis.

HERODS THE GREAT

HEROD THE GREAT
37–4 B.C. (Matt. 2:1)

Mariamne the Hasmonean
- Aristobulus (m) Berenice (d) of Salome sister of Herod the Great
  - HEROD OF CHALCIS (m) Berenice (d) of AGRIPPA I
  - AGRIPPA I 41 – 44 A.D. (Acts 12)
    - AGRIPPA II (Acts 25:13)
    - Berenice (Acts 25:13) (m2) HEROD OF CHALCIS
    - Drusilla (m2) Felix (Acts 24:24)

Mariamne (2)
- Herod-Philip (m) Herodias (Matt. 14:3) (Matt. 14:3)
  - Salome (Matt. 14:6)

Malthace
- ARCHELAUS 4 B.C. – 6 A.D. (Matt. 2:22)
- HEROD ANTIPAS 4 B.C. – 39 A.D. (m) Herodias (Matt. 14)

Cleopatra
- PHILIP THE TETRARCH 4 B.C. – 34 A.D. (Luke 3:1) (m) Salome (Matt. 14:6)

ROMAN GOVERNORS OF JUDEA TO 70 A.D.

Judea was incorporated into the Roman Province of Syria on the deposition of Archelaus as ethnarch in 6 A.D. From that date until the Jewish war with Rome, with the exception of the period 41-44 when Agrippa I was Jewish king, Judea and Samaria were governed by a succession of Roman procurators who were immediately responsible to the Legate of Syria.

Procurators of Judea

COPONIUS (6–9 A.D.)

MARCUS AMBIBULUS (9–11)
ANNIUS RUFUS (12–14)
VALERIUS GRATUS (15–26)

PONTIUS PILATUS (26–36) (Luke 3:1)
MARCELLUS (36–37)
MARULLUS (37–41)
(Agrippa I, Jewish King)
CUSPIUS FADUS (44–46)
TIBERIUS ALEXANDER (46–48)
VENTIDIUS CUMANUS (48–52)
ANTONIUS FELIX (52–60) (Acts 23:24)
PORCIUS FESTUS (60–62) (Acts 24:27)
ALBINUS (62–64)
GESSIUS FLORUS (64–66)
(Vespasian, Commander and Governor of Judea during the war until 69)

Legates of Syria

P. SULPICIUS QUIRINIUS (6–7 A.D.) (Luke 2:2)

Q. CAECILIUS SILANUS (12–17)
CN. CALPURNIUS PISO (17–19)
CN. SENTIUS SATURNINUS (19–21)

L. AELIUS LAMIA (? dates)
L. POMPONIUS FLACCUS (32–35)
L. VITELLIUS (35–39)
P. PETRONIUS (39–42)
MARSUS (42–44)
C. CASSIUS LONGINUS (45–50)

G. UMMIDIUS QUADRATUS (50–60)

GN. DOMITIUS CORBULO (60–63)

C. CESTIUS GALLUS (63–66)

C. LICINIUS MUCIANUS (68–69)

PART X

REFERENCE INDEX

The arrangement of this book makes a general index unnecessary since the matters considered are listed alphabetically in most of the Parts under the subjects treated. A number of directions are also given in the text to enable the reader readily to find additional information on particular themes. But the descriptions accompanying the items and the survey covered by Part IV furnish allusions which are not otherwise listed distinctly. As it may be of service to know what these are, and where they occur, the references have been brought together here as a supplement to the alphabetical scheme.